If?
Then!

CONDITIONS AND PROMISES OF GOD

Carol Morris, PhD.

NEWMAN SPRINGS PUBLISHING
320 Broad Street
Red Bank, NJ 07701

First originally published by Newman Springs Publishing 2021

ISBN 978-1-63692-947-7 (Paperback)
ISBN 978-1-63692-948-4 (Digital)

Printed in the United States of America

Endorsements

I have known Carol Morris for more than twenty years, as her pastor and as her friend. She is a woman with a singular devotion to Jesus Christ and His Word. God has used her to assist an untold number of people to find their way in following Christ. She consistently directs these folks to build their lives upon the truths found in Scripture, not just knowing them but obeying them as well.

In the book *If? Then!*, Carol continues to direct those who will listen to construct a life established on God's powerful Word and fashioned by its principles. Prepare to be blessed by a holy avalanche of God's instructions and promises!

Rev. Lance Lecocq
Senior Pastor
Monroeville Assembly of God

It gives me great pleasure to write my reflections on this wonderful treatise presented to the body of Christ by the mighty servant of God Reverend Carol Morris. This book is just not another book to sit on your shelf, but it has come from the pen of a person whose journey of faith for the last forty years can be summarized as a walk from faith to most holy faith, from glory to glory, and from strength to strength. I have known this great servant of the Lord for the last seven years, and in her, I have seen a person filled with the genuine love of Jesus, unsinkable faith in Christ, unspeakable joy of the Lord, daring to believe God for the impossible. Her life has immensely blessed me, my wife, and children. As I heard her testimony, my love, respect, and honor for this mighty servant of God reached to another height. God has used Reverend Morris to lead many from the ditches of depression, horror of hopelessness, abuse of addiction, and snare of sin to the amazing hope and joy promised by our Lord and Savior, Jesus Christ.

My hope and prayer is that as you read this book, *If? Then!,* your faith in the Lord Jesus Christ and His unfailing promises will remain steadfast and continue to grow.

In Christ Jesus,
Pastor Abraham Simon

To God, who inspired the writing of this book;
my husband, Jack, for his support; and to potential
readers to be blessed by this book.

Acknowledgments

To God the Father, the Lord Jesus Christ, and the Holy Spirit because without them giving me the topic and inspiration to write, this book would never have been written. They challenged me to do something I have never done before. With their guidance, I was able to obediently complete this mission.

I also dedicate this book to my faithful husband, Jack, who patiently endured all the time I needed to spend working on the book. He tirelessly helped me with all the computer challenges in the process of getting it edited.

A grateful thank-you to Pastor Lance Lecocq, who was instrumental in giving this book a title.

A thank-you to my dear family and friends who constantly prayed for me and encouraged me during the times I struggled to believe I could actually write a book.

Finally, I want to thank all the people who will read this book. I pray that God will bless you with a fresh desire to know Him and His Word. May you have new insight into the conditions and promises of God and come to a deeper understanding of the Promiser.

Contents

Introduction

The main purpose of this book is to assist those who seek God, the Promiser, in a deeper way and to remind us that the promises of God have conditions that must be obeyed so that we will receive the many benefits and blessings of God that enrich our lives. We need help to avoid the consequences His promises may contain when we are disobedient. We love to rely on the promises of God but too often ignore or don't pay attention to the conditions, and consequently, we wonder why God hasn't given us what we feel He has promised. As a result, we may feel disappointed with God. There is a cause and an effect to everything in life. We will always reap what we sow. There are always consequences, whether good or bad, to our words and actions. It is the will of God for us to be blessed with His good promises, and He gives us His grace to help us accomplish the conditions. We do not achieve these accomplishments on our own but rather achieve them through the power of the Holy Spirit, our Helper and the One who leads us into all truth. If we focus our mind and loving heart on the Promiser, then we will not have a problem obeying the conditions to receive His blessings and gifts. It is important to remember that the promises may unfold as a more gradual process; this knowledge will ensure that we are ready for God's promises. It is best to wait for God's perfect timing.

Dr. David Jeremiah, author and founder of Turning Point Radio and Television Ministries, and pastor of Shadow Mountain Church, said he knew a man who read his Bible twenty-six times and checked off all the promises of God he found. The twenty-seventh time Jeremiah's friend read the Bible, he counted all the promises he found—they totaled 7,485. This book contains a portion of those promises in the hope that once you have been introduced to them, you will want to search out the other promises that God has made for you. This journey is like a wonderful treasure hunt that will bless you beyond all you could possibly imagine.

According to 1 Kings 8:56, "The Lord has not failed one word of His good promise, which He promised His servant Moses." That same promise stands true for us today. Jesus is the same yesterday, today, and forever (Hebrews 13:8).

Broken promises are painful and regrettable. Have you ever made a promise that you did not keep and then regretted the pain you may have caused someone else because you failed to keep your word? Has someone made a promise to you that they broke? We don't have to worry about broken promises where God is concerned because the Bible is filled with testimonies of the dependability of His words. His words are true and eternal because they reflect His own character.

The decisions you make concerning being obedient to the conditions that God places on His promises have a powerful impact on His destiny for your life. You will reap what you sow.

To help in our understanding and clarification of the meanings of the words promises, conditions, consequences, if, and then, the following definitions are taken from *Webster's American Dictionary*:

- *Promise*: an agreement to do or not to do something; vow to make or keep a promise; a sign that gives reason for expecting success; cause for hope
- *Condition*: anything that must be or must happen before something else can take place
- *If*: "in case that," "supposing that," "on the condition that"
- *Then*: "at that time," "soon afterward," "next in time," "next in order of place"
- *Consequences*: a result or outcome

We do not always receive the promises or the consequences immediately. There may be a time of testing to see how faithful we will be with the promise. Sometimes when people hurt us, it seems like they have gotten away with it, but there will be a time when they will pay for the offense. No one gets away with wrong acts because the Lord will avenge the wrong in His timing. We need to be diligent in waiting on the Lord and trust that His promises will come to fruition in our lives.

The enemy will try to discourage you and lie to you that God will never give you the promise. An example of those who were diligent in waiting is Abraham and Sarah in the book of Genesis, who were waiting for a son. It took years before that promise manifested. Sometimes God waits until He is the only way that the promise can happen. This is the time our faith is tested to see if we really believe and trust our Lord.

If you are waiting on God, wait without wavering. He is never late; He always keeps His promises. He is always true to His Word. His timing is perfect.

Irish clergyman Robert Traill said, "We find…that the promises that are the ground of the Christian's faith are the promises of the Father, as the Author… We find the promises ascribed unto Jesus Christ, and He is the Promiser. When He left His people and went out of this world, He left them with the…abundance of promises… The promises are also given by the Holy Spirit; He is called the 'Spirit of Promise.'"

Together they make and keep every promise in the Bible. God the Father ordains them, Christ purchased them for us with His blood, the Holy Spirit brings them to fruition in our daily lives. Broken promises are the source of pain here on earth, but God never changes. His promises are as sure as His unchanging nature; and they are tripled in power, for they come from God the Father, God the Son, and God the Holy Spirit.

IF? THEN! POEM

The use of the word "IF" contains so much power
It can change your life from hour to hour
The impact it has covers a very wide range
It can cause a very good or very bad change
Relying on "IFS" and "BUTS" to make a decision
Can bring about much indecision
Too many "IFS" can cause you to doubt
Of the good things in life you may miss out
Minding the conditions can bring a prosperous life
Ignoring conditions will bring unhappy strife
Consequences are followed by the word "THEN"
Either bringing happiness or sadness again
When we make a choice, there is always a cause and effect
So make sure you seek the wisdom of God and let him direct
If we all want to benefit from the good promises of God we want to
      acquire
Our focus should be on the Promiser, and it is Him we should desire
If it is the Promiser rather than the promise that we seek
THEN God will give us all the promises we need in life to have and
      to speak.

I have adapted the following promises, conditions, and consequences from selected books of *The Prayer Bible* by Elmer L. Towns
and Roy B. Zuck (Liberty University Press, 2014).

You might want to personalize the Word of God by praying
the Scriptures—over your life. Praying them out loud is powerful
because faith comes by hearing and hearing by the Word of God.
God loves when we pray His Word back to Him. There is power
in the Word of God. These Scriptures are powerful to meditate on
and to speak over your life. The Word of God is powerful and can
transform you when you apply the prayers to your life. Application
of God's Word is needed to transform your life. Applying His Word
makes you a doer of the Word and not just one who hears it.

The Lord gave me this word concerning the Scriptures: He said: "Information without application is nullification, but information with application brings revelation and transformation." If you just read the Word of God without applying it, then all you have is more information without the life-changing power it contains.

Book of Matthew

If your tree does not bear good fruit, then it is cut down by the ax of God's judgment and thrown into the fire. (Matthew 3:10)

If you repent and are willing to change your inner self and that which was your old way of thinking, regret your sin, and live a changed life. I, John the Baptist, will baptize you with water, then the Messiah, Jesus, will baptize you who truly repent with the Holy Spirit, but if you remain unrepentant, then Jesus will baptize you with fire—meaning His judgment. (Matthew 3:11)

If you are a believer, Jesus will gather you into His kingdom, but if you are unrepentant, then He will burn up the chaff with unquenchable fire. (Matthew 3:12)

If you are poor in spirit, meaning those devoid of spiritual arrogance, who regard themselves as insignificant, then you are blessed, spiritually prosperous, happy, to be admired, and the kingdom of heaven is yours both now and forever. (Matthew 5:3)

If you mourn over your sins and repent, then you will be blessed, forgiven, refreshed by God's grace and you are comforted when the burden of sin is lifted. (Matthew 5:4)

If you are inwardly peaceful, spiritually secure, worthy of respect, gentle, kind-hearted, sweet-spirited, and self-controlled, then you are blessed and inherit the earth. (Matthew 5:5)

If you hunger and thirst for righteousness and actively seek right standing with God, then you are blessed, joyful, nourished by God's goodness and will be completely satisfied. (Matthew 5:6)

If you are merciful, then you will be blessed, content, sheltered by God's promises and will receive mercy. (Matthew 5:7)

If you are pure in heart with integrity, moral courage, and Godly character, then you are blessed with anticipating God's presence, spiritually mature, and you will see God. (Matthew 5:8)

If you are a peacemaker and are building relationships with others, then you will be called a child of God. (Matthew 5:9)

If you are persecuted for doing that which is morally right, then you will be blessed and comforted with God's love, and yours is the kingdom of heaven both now and forever. (Matthew 5:10)

If people insult you and persecute you, falsely say all kinds of evil things against you because of your association with Jesus, then you are blessed, morally courageous, and spiritually alive; there is joy in God's goodness. (Matthew 5:11)

If you let your light shine before men in such a way that they may see your good deeds and moral excellence, then they will recognize, honor, and glorify your Father who is in heaven. (Matthew 5:16)

If you break one of the least of these commandments, and teach others to do the same, then you will be called least important in the kingdom of heaven; but if you practice and teach them the commandments, then you will be called great in the kingdom of heaven. (Matthew 5:19)

If your righteousness, uprightness, and moral excellence are not more than the Scribes and Pharisees, then you will never enter the kingdom of heaven. (Matthew 5:20)

If you continue to be angry or harbor malice against your brother, then you shall be guilty before the court. If you speak contemptuously and insultingly to your brother, saying Raca, which means: you empty-headed idiot, you shall be guilty before the Supreme Court. If you say, "You fool," then you shall be in danger of the fiery hell. (Matthew 5:22)

If you do good deeds publicly to be seen by men, then you will have no reward prepared and awaiting you with your Father who is in Heaven. (Matthew 6:1)

If when you pray, you go into your most private room, close the door and pray to your Father who sees what is done in secret, then He will reward you. (Matthew 6:6)

If you forgive others their trespasses of their reckless and willful sins, then your heavenly Father will also forgive you. If you do not forgive others by nurturing your hurt and anger, resulting in it interfering with your relationship with God, then your Father will not forgive your trespasses. (Matthew 6:14–15)

If you fast not to be noticed by men but only by your Father who is in secret, then your Father who sees in secret will reward you. (Matthew 6:18)

If your eye, which is the lamp of the body, is clear and spiritually perceptive, then your whole body will be full of light benefiting from God's precepts. If your eye is bad, spiritually blind, then your whole body will be full of darkness and devoid of God's precepts. (Matthew 6:22–23)

If you first and most importantly seek, aim at, strive after His Kingdom and His righteousness, His way of doing and being right, which is the attitude and character of God, then all these things: food, drink, clothes, etc. will be given to you also. (Matthew 6:33)

If you judge and criticize and condemn others unfairly with an attitude of self-righteous superiority as though assuming the office of a judge, then you will be judged unfairly. If you hypocritically judge others when you are sinful and unrepentant, then you will be judged; if, in accordance with your standard of measure, you pass out judgment, then judgment will be measured to you. (Matthew 7:1–2)

If you ask and keep on asking, then it will be given to you; if you seek and keep on seeking, then you will find; if you knock and keep on knocking, then the door will be opened to you. (Matthew 7:7)

If you hear these words of Jesus and act on them, then you will be a wise man, a far-sighted, practical, and sensible man who built his house on the rock. If you hear these words of Jesus and do not do them, then you will be like a foolish, stupid man who built his house on the sand. (Matthew 7:24–26)

If people from all religions, no matter how sincere or persistent, don't come to the Father through Jesus Christ, then their prayers will not be heard and the only prayer God will answer is when they come to the Father through Jesus Christ and ask God to be merciful to them though they are sinners. (Matthew 7:29)

If you will testify of Jesus before men, then He will testify of you before Jesus' Father in heaven, but if you deny Jesus before men, then He will deny you before His Father in heaven. (Matthew 10:32–33)

If anyone loves father and mother more than Me, then he/she is not worthy of Me, and if anyone is worthy of Me, then he/she must take up their cross and follow Me. (Matthew 10:37–38)

If you do not take your cross, expressing a willingness to endure whatever may come, and follow Jesus, believing in Him, conforming to His example in living and, if need be, suffering or perhaps dying because of faith in Me, then you are not worthy of Me. If whoever finds his life in this world will eventually lose it through death and, if whoever loses his life in this world for My sake will then find it, that is, life with Me for all eternity. (Matthew 10:38–39)

If you come to me when you are tired and carry heavy burdens, then I will give you rest. If you take My yoke, and learn from Me, for I am gentle and humble in heart, then you will find rest for your souls. (Matthew 11:28–29)

If you speak careless words, then you will have to give an account of every careless word that you speak on the Day of Judgment. By your words you will be free and by your words you will be judged. (Matthew 12:36–37)

If you do something for Jesus, then you will be given more till you have plenty. If you do nothing for Jesus, then what you have will be taken away. (Matthew 12:12)

If you hear the message of the kingdom and do not respond, then the devil comes to snatch away the message. If you receive the message but don't understand, then you give up when trouble or persecution comes. If a person hears the message but gives up because of worldly things or pursuit of money, then the truth is choked out and you yield no fruit. If you hear the truth and believe the message, then you bring forth fruit: thirty, sixty or a hundredfold. (Matthew 13:19–22)

If anyone will follow Me, Jesus, then let him take up his cross daily and follow Me. If you try to save your life on this earth, then you will lose it. If you lose your life for My sake, then you will find it. (Matthew 24–25)

If your brother does something wrong, then go to him privately and show where he is wrong. If he listens, then you have won back your brother. If he will not listen, then take one or two others, so that you have witnesses confirmed by their testimony. If he refuses to listen to them, then report the matter to the church, treat him as a pagan and as an abomination. (Matthew 18:15–17)

If you bind anything on earth, then it will be bound in heaven, and if you release anything on earth, it is released in heaven. If only two of you on earth agree on what they ask, then you will receive it from My heavenly Father. (Matthew 18:18–19)

If two or three meet as My disciples, then I am present with them. (Matthew 18:20)

If you want eternal life, then you must continually keep the Ten Commandments. (Matthew 19:17)

If you are going to be perfect, go and sell all that you own and give the money to the poor; then you will have riches in heaven; then come and follow Me. (Matthew 19:21)

If in the new world when the Son of Man shall take His seat on His throne, then you who have followed Me will sit on twelve thrones and rule the twelve tribes of Israel. And everyone who has left home, brothers, sisters, father, mother, children, or land, for My sake, then will be rewarded a hundred times in addition to eternal life. (Matthew 19:28)

If you are last, then you will be first, and those who are first will then be last. (Matthew 20:16)

If you want to be great, then you must be a servant; and if you want to be first, then you must be a slave, just as Jesus came not to be served but to serve, and to give His life as a ransom for many. (Matthew 20:27–28)

If you have faith and do not doubt, then you can do this miracle. You can say to this mountain, "be moved and throw yourself into the sea." Then it will be done. If you have faith, then whatever you ask for in prayer, you will receive. (Matthew 21:21–22)

If you exalt yourself, then you will be humbled. If you humble yourself, then you will be exalted. (Matthew 23:12)

Book of Psalms

If I don't walk according to ungodly counsel, hang out with sinners, or sit with scorners, then I am happily blessed. (Psalm 1:1)

If you are like the ungodly, then you are like the husk the wind blows away, and you shall be punished in God's judgment and shall not enter the congregation of Your people. (Psalm 1:4)

If we trust in Your Son, then we are blessed. (Psalm 2:12)

If I cry out to You for help, then answer me from Your Holy mountain. Selah! (Psalm 3:4)

If I lie down in sleep in peace, then I know I am safe in You. Selah! (Psalm 4:8)

If I look to You and pray in the morning, then I know You will hear me. (Psalm 5:3)

If they sin foolishly, then they cannot enter God's Presence because God hates the iniquity they do. If they do sin foolishly, then He will destroy those who blaspheme because God rejects murders and liars. (Psalm 5:5–6)

If I put my trust in You, then You will destroy enemies and I will constantly shout for joy. (Psalm 5:11)

If you love the Lord, then constantly rejoice in Him because you know God will bless the righteous and constantly defend you. (Psalm 5:12)

If my enemy is a friend of iniquity, then he constantly thinks of harming others. He is always digging a trap, but he falls into his self-made destruction and his attack on others ends up hurting himself; his wounds are self-inflicted. (Psalm 8:14–16)

If I live by the right principles, then You support me Lord because You always support the right thing. (Psalm 9:4)

If you put God first and put your trust in Him, then He will not forsake you. (Psalm 9:10)

If you are unsaved, then you will fall into the evil trap you set for your enemies; you are imprisoned in the cell you prepare for others. The wicked are condemned to the punishment they plan for others. (Psalm 9:15–16)

If you deny the Lord, then you will be put in hell with people who deny the Lord. (Psalm 9:17)

If you are wicked, then you are too proud to seek God; and you never realize you will have to answer to God, because every evil thing they do succeeds and they laugh at their victims. You also boast that you are not going to get hurt and are free to do anything you want. Your mouth is full of cursing and lies; your evil plans are on the tip of your tongue. (Psalm 10:4–7)

If you do right, then the Lord loves and favors you with His Presence because He is a righteous God. (Psalm 11:7)

If you trust in God's Word, then He will keep you and will preserve you from the enemies' lies, even when the enemy is all about you. (Psalm 12:7–8)

If I trust in Your mercy to save me, then I know You will deliver me. And I will worship You with singing, because You will abundantly bless me. (Psalm 13:5–6)

If you are a fool, then you deny that God exists to justify your corrupt lifestyle and don't want to do good. Deniers turn from You and do filthy things and eat up good people like bread, and never call on You. (Psalm 4:1, 3–4)

If you do right, then you are afraid to deny God and don't listen to the enemies but put your trust in the Lord. (Psalm 14:5)

If you want to live with God in His tabernacle in the holy hill, then you follow God's principles, do the right thing, tell the truth, do not lie about others, do not sin against your friends, recognize the enemies of God, don't retaliate, don't charge usury for loans, and don't take bribes. (Psalm 15:1–5)

If you fear His name and live blamelessly for God, then He will honor you. (Psalm 15:5)

If you worship earthly gods, then you will never find peace. (Psalm 16:4)

If I call out to God, then I know He is listening and answers the request that I make. (Psalm 17:6)

If I see Your face, then I will be happy and will be conformed into Your image. (Psalm 17:15)

If I am afraid Lord, then I will call on You; even though You are in Your temple, You will hear me and give attention to my prayers. (Psalm 18:6)

If my enemy almost overwhelms me, then You, Lord, save me. You lifted me into a secure place, and You put Your delight in me. (Psalm 18:18)

If we live by Your principles and separate ourselves from sin, then You come to reward us. You showed mercy to us who received mercy; You judged us righteously who relied on Your righteousness. You showed Yourself pure to those who sought Your purity; You showed Yourself merciful to those who need mercy. You saved those who are sorry for their sin, and punished those who refused to humble themselves. (Psalm 18:20–27)

If I have You, Lord, then I can defeat a troop of men and with Your help, I can jump over a wall. (Psalm 18:29)

If You give me life and strength and salvation, then I bless You and exalt You, Lord. (Psalm 18:46–47)

If I fear You and follow Your never-changing principles, then You take away doubts and ignorance and make me wise, and if I apply Your truth, then I will live forever. (Psalm 19:8–9)

If I obey Your principles, then it is more satisfying than sweets because it keeps me on guard against danger. (Psalm 19:10–11)

If I am unable to perceive my slightest deviation from truth, then keep me from making ignorant mistakes and making presumptuous errors because I don't want to be controlled by my faults. I want to live blamelessly by Your principles so that I will be kept from making life-destroying decisions. (Psalm 19:12–13)

If you save me, then I will rejoice and tell everyone what You have done and that You have carried out Your will in my life. (Psalm 20:5)

If I trust in Your name, Lord, then my enemies will be defeated and eliminated and I will be vindicated and stand before You. (Psalm 20:7–8)

If you worship the Lord, then He will come to you; and if you trust Him during troubled times, then He leads you through your troubled times;

and if you cry for deliverance, then He will give you great victories. (Psalm 22:3–5)

If we trust God, then You will come to us when we are in trouble, You will not hide Your face from us when we need You and we will praise You to other believers. (Psalm 22:24)

If we will do everything that we promised, then weak Christians will be encouraged to trust You, and they will continue following You throughout their lives. (Psalm 22:25–26)

If you are part of the small remnant who serve God, then you are the ones God recognizes and protects and You will declare to all how You take care of Your children; and each new generation will contain more believers who will also declare Your goodness and care. (Psalm 22:30–31)

If You are my Shepherd Lord, then I don't need anything because you make me lie down in green pastures, You lead me beside still waters, You renew my spiritual energy, You guide me in the right paths to glorify Your name. (Psalm 23:1–3)

If I walk through dark valleys, then I will not be afraid of death shadows because You are with me; Your rod and staff protect me. You prepare a banquet table for me, and my enemies watch me eat. You pour oil on my head to honor and heal me; You fill my cup so it runs over. Surely Your goodness and mercy will follow me as long as I live on this earth; and in eternity I will live in Your house forever. (Psalm 23:4–6)

If you have clean hands and a pure heart, and separate yourself from sin, then you can come into the presence of the Lord and you are able to stand before Him. (Psalm 24:3–4)

If you stand in His presence, then you will receive blessings and He will declare you righteous through salvation because you are the ones who seek to know Him and want to stand in His presence. (Psalm 24:5–6)

If they will fear Your name, then You will guide them to do right things; give them peace because of their obedience and You will let their children prosper. (Psalm 25:12–13)

If they obey Him, then He agrees to give life to them. (Psalm 25:14)

If I always look to You for deliverance, then You will lead me through trouble. (Psalm 25:15)

If I always try to live innocently, then I walk in Your forgiveness. I tell every one I am thankful for You, and I am grateful for Your work in my life. (Psalm 26:6–7)

If troubles and problems attack me, then You will hide me in Your presence and set me on a rock so my enemies can't reach me. (Psalm 27:5)

If you lift me up above my enemies, Lord, then I will bring the sacrifices of joy to You and sing praises to You. (Psalm 27:6)

If I pray to You for help, then don't be silent. If You don't hear and answer my prayer, then I'll be like the unsaved who can't pray. (Psalm 28:1)

If all of us enjoy this earth, then we are obliged to worship You because it reflects the beauty of Your holiness. (Psalm 29:2)

If the storms rage in your life, then the Lord gives you strength to live through them and gives you inner peace while the storms rage. (Psalm 29:11)

If I am sick, I beg You to let me live; then You healed me, delivered me from dying and kept me alive for Your purpose. (Psalm 30:2–3)

If I obey You Lord, then You are so good to me, so I trust You with my reputation. (Psalm 31:9)

If You, Lord, protect me from all kinds of danger, then I bless You for Your mercy. (Psalm 31:21)

If I put my hope in You, then You make me courageous in the face of lies and strengthen me to deal with them, so I love You for protecting me and for punishing those who lie about me. (Psalm 31:23–24)

If you forgive all my rebellion, cover my sin, erase my errors from Your books and don't remember them, then I am blessed and can enjoy Your Presence. (Psalm 32:1–2)

If I refuse to recognize my sin, then my whole body cries out with conviction. If I confess my transgression to You and repent, then You forgive my terrible sin. (Psalm 32:3, 5)

If You are gracious to forgive our iniquity, then every godly person will rest securely in You when judgment comes on us. (Psalm 2:6)

If you rebel against God, then you have a hard life, but God shows mercy to those who trust Him, and I am happy because I follow Your principles and I shout for joy because You make me do right. (Psalm 32:10–11)

If You allow me to approach You, then I rejoice and worship You as I come to You. (Psalm 33:1)

If the ungodly go against Your principles, then You, Lord, mess up their plans because Your decisions are always right. (Psalm 33:10–11)

If any group follows Your laws, then You will always bless them and make them Your people. (Psalm 33:12)

If we reverently follow You and trust in Your mercy, then You will deliver our souls from hell and take care of us on this earth. (Psalm 33:18–19)

If I am scared, then I cry to You for help and You hear me and deliver me from all my troubles. (Psalm 34:6)

If you don't want to die but live and have a good life, then you must quit speaking evil and begin seeking the truth found in You, and repent of your evil ways and live peacefully according to God's principles. (Psalm 34:12–14)

If you live right and cry to the Lord, then the Lord delivers you out of all your troubles. He is near to those who have a broken heart and He saves those who are sorry for their sin. (Psalm 34:17–18)

If you hate peace-loving people, then you will never have peace and sinners will agonize over their sins. (Psalm 34:21)

If You, Lord, save me from my enemies, then I rejoice in You and thank You deeply for delivering me from any enemy who was too strong for me. (Psalm 35:9–10)

If arrogant people attack and try to destroy you, then they will fail because of their sin and when they die, they will not live in Your presence. (Psalm 36:11–12)

If you are a lawbreaker, then you will soon dry up like cut grass and will eventually die just like new flowers eventually wither. (Psalm 37:2)

If I put my trust in You and live right, then I know You will protect me and provide for me and You satisfy me more than anything else and You fulfill every desire of my heart. (Psalm 37:3–4)

If I commit my days' activities to You, then I know You will work everything out. (Psalm 37:5)

If you are meek, then you will be rewarded by God and will live happy and secure lives. (Psalm 37:11)

If the wicked make elaborate plans to defraud Your followers and steal everything they possess, then You will use their cheating ways against them and they will lose everything they have stolen. (Psalm 37:14–15)

If you are God's children, then He takes care of you and gives you a reward you will never lose and you will not be ashamed when God judges you and He will provide for you in difficult times. (Psalm 37:18–19)

If you delight to follow God's principles, then God will direct your steps and good people do not stay down when knocked down because You help them get up each time. (Psalm 37:23–24)

If you do right, then God loves you and will never forsake you if you follow Him and you will inherit the earth one day and live there forever with Him; he will always say the right things and will tell everyone that You do right things. They will live by Your laws; your feet will not be tripped up by sin. (Psalm 37:28–31

If you do right and trust in God, then God will save and strengthen you when trouble comes, help you make it through difficult times, and deliver you from wicked ones. (Psalm 37:39–40)

If you look after the poor, then the Lord blesses you and promises to deliver you who defend the poor and will preserve your life and You will not deliver them to their enemies. If you get sick, then God will take care of you and be with you in your illness. (Psalm 41:1–3)

If you raise me up from my sickness, then it will be a signal that my enemies cannot defeat me. (Psalm 41:11)

If I want You to refresh me again, then I must drink daily from Your love to me and must worship You each night with songs and prayer. (Psalm 42:7–8)

If I can't come close to You in the temple, then I feel lost in the darkness and my enemies laugh at my commitment to You. If I am discouraged in my soul and my spirit is sad, then I will worship You in my heart because You strengthen my confidence, my Lord and my God. (Psalm 42:9–11)

If I want to make good decisions, then I need You to give me the light of Your wisdom. (Psalm 43:3)

If I come to the altar to confess my sin, then I will happily come to You and joyfully sing Your praises. (Psalm 43:4)

If everything goes badly for us, then we will not forget You and will not stop obeying You. Our heart is not hardened against You and we have not quit following You even though You let our enemies punish us and let the shadow of death fall over us. We have not forgotten the power of

Your name, nor have we stretched out our hands to false gods. (Psalm 44:17–20)

If I have trouble, then You are my refuge and strength and are present to help when I have trouble. (Psalm 46:1)

If I want to learn to know You intimately, then I will be still in Your presence. (Psalm 46:10)

If you think you will never die, then you are not smart, and will be remembered as a fool. (Psalm 49:13)

If wicked people are rich, then it doesn't bother me nor do I care that they live in big expensive houses because they can't take it with them when they die. They will die like everyone else, but they shall not see the light of Your presence. (Psalm 49:16, 19)

If we worship You honestly, then You accept and save us. (Psalm 50:23)

If You cleanse me from my sins, then I can be clean and if You wash me, then I can be whiter than snow. (Psalm 51:7)

If You keep me from the death penalty for my sin and rescue me and save me, then I will rejoice in Your forgiveness, my lips will sing forth Your mercy, and praise Your grace. (Psalm 51:14–15)

If I have the inward sacrifice of a broken, contrite and repentant heart, then You will not reject me. (Psalm 51:7)

If they are a lying people, then the Lord will destroy them and separate them from His presence and they will not receive eternal life. (Psalm 52:5)

If you are a fool, then you say God does not exist because of your corruption. (Psalm 3:1)

If they are sinners, then they don't understand their sin and never call on God and they will be terrorized by God when He judges them for their sin because they have despised Him. (Psalm 53:4–5)

If my trouble came from an outside enemy, then I could deal with it better. But my trouble comes from an insider, a person I thought was my friend. (Psalm 55:12, 14)

If I call upon You Lord, then I know You will save me. I will pray to You evening, morning, and noon because I know You will hear me. (Psalm 55:16)

If I cast my burdens on You, then I know You will sustain me because You will never permit the righteous to be destroyed. (Psalm 55:22)

If I am most afraid, then I will trust in Your protection and will exalt Your Word that protects me. (Psalm 56:3–4)

If I cry to You, then my enemies are stopped; therefore I know You are for me. (Psalm 56:9)

If You protect me from destruction and keep the evil one from me, then I will praise You for safety. (Psalm 56:12–13)

If I cry unto You, O God, Most High, then You will fulfill Your plan for me and send help from heaven to save me from my enemy that would destroy me and You show me Your love and faithfulness. (Psalm 57:2–3)

If you are sinful people, then you lie from your birth and lie as sure as they are born. Your words are like a serpent's venom; and you stop up your ears to any pleas. (Psalm 58:3–4)

If You defend me from my enemies and protect me in time of trouble, then I will sing of Your power and every morning I will sing of Your love. (Psalm 59:16

If we fear You, then we can rally to Your banner because it is displayed because of Your truth. (Psalm 60:4)

If my salvation comes from You, then I wait for You to give me rest because only You are my Rock and Salvation; my fortress when I am shaken. I find my rest in You, my hope is only in You. You alone are my rock and salvation, my fortress where I am secure. My salvation and hope come from You; hide me in a rock where I will be safe. Lord, I trust in You at all times; I pour out my heart to You because You are my refuge. Selah! (Psalm 62:5–8)

If there are those that scheme to destroy me, then they will die and be buried. They will die by the sword and scavengers will eat their remains. (Psalm 63:9–10)

If they realize what You have done, then the righteous will rejoice in You and Your people will praise You and everyone will fear You because You will shoot arrows at them and suddenly they shall be wounded and all their supporters will abandon them. (Psalm 64:7–10)

If we are chosen by God, then we are blessed and come into His presence, dwell in Your courts, and are satisfied with Your goodness, even living in Your Holy Temple. (Psalm 65:4)

If God allows the enemy to ride roughshod over us and be tested with fire and water, then God will bring us out into a wealthy place. (Psalm 66:12)

If my thoughts were motivated by sin, then You would not have heard me; but You did hear me when I cried, and You listened to my request. I praise You for not neglecting my prayer and not quitting loving me. (Psalm 66:18–20)

If You will be merciful to us and bless us, let Your face shine on us; let Your way be known on earth and Your prosperity known by all people, then all people will worship You with praise; yes, all people will worship You and be glad and joyfully sing because You will examine everyone correctly and rule them properly. (Psalm 67:1–4)

If I sing praises to You, O God, then I magnify You who rides the heavens. I rejoice in Your name Jehovah; You are a father to the fatherless. You are a protective judge to the widows; You give us all a family. You set the captives free but You punish the rebellious. (Psalm 68:4–6)

If we bless You, our Lord of salvation, then You load us with good things. Selah! You are the God of salvation who rescues us from death. (Psalm 68:19–20)

If we belong to You, then we will taste victory and see Your victory parade as You march triumphantly into Your sanctuary. (Psalm 68:24)

If I continue to pray to You, O Lord, then You will eventually listen to me. In your great mercy you will hear me and save me from all my troubles, deliver me from being stuck in the mud and not let me sink any further. You will deliver me from those who hate me and from deep waters of trouble. You won't let circumstances overwhelm me and not allow death to swallow me up. (Psalm 69:13–15)

If You deliver me to solid ground when I am suffering from much pain, then I will sing praises to Your name; I will magnify You with Thanksgiving. (Psalm 69:29–30)

If you are humble, then you will recognize what He is doing and those who seek You will the live better lives. (Psalm 69:32)

If you seek the Lord's protection, then you will find joy in His presence. (Psalm 70:4)

If You do not forsake me now that I'm old and gray-headed, then I will tell the next generation about Your power so those growing up will know Your miracles. Psalm 71:18)

If You allow me to suffer many ways, then You will resurrect me from the grave and You will restore my life to me; You will again honor me in the future and comfort me with Your kindness. (Psalm 71:20–21)

If you are righteous, then you will flourish under Him and there will be peace as long as the moon endures. (Psalm 72:7)

If you are needy and poor, then He will deliver the needy from trouble and help the poor out of their calamity; He will give to the needy and He will reward the poor; He will save them from death and their life will be precious to Him. (Psalm 72:12–14)

If they will not follow the Lord, then they will perish because God will destroy those who reject Him. (Psalm 73:27)

If you follow the Lord's command to teach the law to your children, then the coming genera-tions will know the law, even their children not yet born, so they in turn will tell their children with the result that they would trust You, O God; then the coming generations would not forget Your works but keep the commands You have given so they would not be like their forefathers who were a stubborn and rebellious generation who refused to yield their hearts to You, whose spirits did not want to obey You. (Psalm 78:5–8)

If we would just open ourselves to You, then You promised to fill our lives. (Psalm 81:10)

If we would not listen to Your voice and we would not yield to Your leadership, then You give us over to our sinful hearts; You let us make our own decisions. (Psalm 81:11–12)

If we would have just listened to You and obeyed Your principles, then You would have defeated our enemies and strengthened our hand against our foes. (Psalm 81:13)

If those who hate You would have feared You because You would have punished them, then You would have fed us with the best food and satisfied us with honey from the rock. (Psalm 81:15–16)

If you realize Your strength is in the Lord because Your principles are in your heart, then He will bless you. (Psalm 84:5)

If I walk uprightly, then Lord, You will shine warmth on my life like the sun; You protect me like a shield; You will not withhold any good thing from me. (Psalm 84:11)

If we fear You, then You will surely save us so Your glory can live in the land. (Psalm 85:9)

If You teach me the way I should walk, then I will follow Your truth. If You give me a focused heart, then I will fear Your name and praise You with my whole heart, O Lord my God; I will glorify Your name forever. (Psalm 86:11–12)

If I make You my protective refuge, then O Lord, no harm can destroy me because You will command Your angels to guard me in all ways, they will protect me with their hands to keep me from falling. (Psalm 91:9–12)

If I love you Lord, then You will protect me from danger and if I know You by name, then You will be with me in trouble. If I call on You for help, then You will answer me. You will be with me, protect me and my honor; You will give me long life and satisfy me with Your salvation. (Psalm 91:14–16)

If you are righteous, then you will flourish like a palm tree; you will grow like the cedars of Lebanon. If you are planted in God's house, then you will flourish in His courts; you will bear fruit in your old age and will stay fruitful and green. And your life will testify that God is just, He is your Rock, and He is always good to His people. (Psalm 92:12–15)

If I am overwhelmed with anxiety, then Your comfort gives me peace and joy. (Psalm 94:19)

If you worship idols, then you will be ashamed; those who glory in their idols will recognize Your majestic glory. (Psalm 97:7)

If there are those who slander their friends, then I will turn my back on them. If they are selfish and proud, then I will have nothing to do with them. (Psalm 101:4–5)

If you are deceitful, then you will not dwell with God, and those who lie and rebel, will not stand in Your presence. (Psalm 101:7)

If I fear You and delight in Your Word, then I praise You for blessing me. (Psalm 112:1)

If my children do right, then You have promised my children will be influential and You will bless them. (Psalm 112:2)

If I continually live righteously, then You have promised to bless me with wealth and riches. (Psalm 112:3)

If I am upright as a light in the darkness and am gracious and compassionate to all, graciously give to the needy, and guide my life with truth, then I shall not be shaken and my righteousness will be remembered forever. (Psalm 112:4–6)

If you create idols and make them like yourself and trust idols, then you are only worshiping yourself. (Psalm 15:8)

If you are faithful to God to the end, then you are precious to God when you die. (Psalm 116:15)

If my enemies have me hemmed in, then I will defeat them in Your name. (Psalm 118:11)

If You open the gates of righteousness for me, then I will enter to give thanks to You, O Lord. (Psalm 118:19)

If you are blameless and walk according to God's law, keep His statutes and seek Him with all your heart, and do not commit iniquity but walk according to His way, then God will bless you. (Psalm 119:1–3)

If you know and obey God's Word, then a young man can keep clean. (Psalm 119:9)

If You bless me, then I may live before You and keep the Word You have given. (Psalm 119:17)

If I didn't have the encouragement of Your law, then I would have given in to my affliction. (Psalm 119:92)

If troubles and anxiety overwhelm me, then Your commands get me through problems. (Psalm 119:143)

If rulers persecute me without cause, then my heart still respects Your Word. (Psalm 119:161)

If You, Lord, had not been on my side when my enemies attacked me, then they would have swallowed me alive because their anger was so hot against me. The waters would have drowned me; the torrent would have flooded my soul and the angry waters from the storm would have overwhelmed my life. (Psalm 124:2–5)

If You kept a record of our sin, then no one could stand before You, but there is forgiveness with You so that we fear You. (Psalm 130:3)

If Your people sin, then You will judge them and forgive them when they repent. (Psalm 135:14)

If I call to You in trouble, then You answer by encouraging me with Your strength. (Psalm 138:3)

If I could go to heaven, then You are there; if I make my bed in hell, then You are there. If I could fly away on the wings of a new day and fly across the sea, then even there I would find Your hand guiding me and Your right hand holding me. (Psalm 139:8–10)

If I could count all of them, then Your thoughts of me are more than the grains of the sand. (Psalm 139:18)

If You will do the right thing to the poor and protect the rights of the needy, then the godly will praise Your name and they will live in Your presence forever. (Psalm 140:12–13)

If I stray and am stubborn, then let Godly people remind me and rebuke me and make me listen to them. (Psalm 141:5)

If we call on You, then You are near to us and to those who sincerely seek Your presence. (Psalm 145:18)

If we fear You, then You satisfy our desires and You will hear our cry and save us. (Psalm 145:19)

If you are oppressed, then God will protect you; give food to the hungry and set the prisoners free. (Psalm 146:7–8)

If You take pleasure in Your people, then make the humble beautiful with salvation. (Psalm 149:4)

Book of Proverbs

If you gain much counsel from the wise, then you can become a smart person and learn to understand things that are difficult. (Proverbs 1:6)

If I destroy the lives of other people, then I am really condemning my own life. (Proverbs 1:12)

If we return to You when You call, You promise to pour Your Spirit on us and to teach us Your ways. (Proverbs 1:23)

If he rebels when you call to him and stretch out Your hand to him, rejects Your ways and is determined to do the exact opposite and completely rejects all You stand for, then You will turn Your back when he is punished and say: "You got what you wanted." Then the rebel will be scared to death and the consequences of his sin rip him apart when he cries out in anguish. He'll cry out for mercy, but will not get it; he'll seek You but You'll not be found. There is no second chance in hell because the rebel hated Your way of life and would not listen and learn from You. He rejected Your plans for his life and refused to do what You wanted him to do. (Proverbs 1:24–30)

If you sin, then you bear the consequences of that sin and shall suffer the misery you give others and your vile trespass shall be your own punishment. If you listen and learn from God's instructions, then you shall be safe in His Presence, and shall be delivered from evil. (Proverbs 1:31, 33)

If you seek to live the right way, then there is abundant wisdom for you and the Lord protects those who know Him, and who attempt to walk the right way. If you make right decisions, then God will show you the right paths. If you honestly seek to do the right thing, then God's Spirit helps you to know what to do, and He guides you in good paths. If you experience God's wisdom, then God directs your life correctly and you enjoy fellowship with Him and you don't make bad decisions or make mistakes and evil people don't take advantage of you, nor do they talk you into making bad decisions. (Proverbs 2:6–12)

If you obey His wisdom, then you are headed toward eternal life. If you follow His principles, then you will enter into fellowship with God and may stay there as long as you obey Him. But the rebellious will eventually die and not enjoy fellowship with God. (Proverbs 2:20–22)

If you let God's principles control your thought processes, then God will add value to your life and others will respect your commitment to truth. (Proverbs 3:4)

If you will trust in God with all your heart, not lean on your own way of doing things, not make decisions apart from God, in all your actions acknowledge Him, then He will direct your paths. If you choose not to do things your own way nor prize your opinions over God's, and reverence God in all you do and separate yourself from all appearances of evil, then your paths shall make you wise and healthy and God's ways shall make you strong. (Proverbs 3:7–8)

If you get wisdom, apply it to your life and make understanding first in your life and honor the pursuit of wisdom, then it will make you first in the lives of others and will make you honorable. (Proverbs 4:7–9)

If you do right, then your path gets brighter every day and leads toward the shining light. If you do wicked things, then your path gets darker all the time, and eventually you will stumble in the night. If I do not turn away from His counsel nor refuse to listen to His direction, then His instructions will make things easier and will enrich all I do in life. (Proverbs 4:18–19)

If You will help me listen to wise advice and understand helpful counsel, then I may learn life-improving principles and not forget beneficial truth. (Proverbs 5:1–2)

If I drink from my own well and do not sacrifice my life to the lust of the flesh and preserve my own self-esteem and not give it away, then You will bless my decisions and I will rejoice with my spouse. He/she will give me comfort and strength and I will be happy with him/her and we will be happy with each other. (Proverbs 5:15–19)

If we sin against You, then we shall be a prisoner to our iniquity; our lust shall become our punishment. We shall die without knowing anything better, and the greatest consequence of our sin is that it drives us away from You. (Proverbs 5:22–23)

If I co-sign a friend's loan, or shake hands on a bad deal, then my agreement will become a trap and my words will come back to haunt me. If I get out of every bad arrangement, then I won't lose my friends when they try to take advantage of me. (Proverbs 6:1–3)

If we obey Your words, then no one will go astray who obeys. (Proverbs 8:8)

If I ask You for Your wisdom, then it will lead me to do the appropriate thing, and will help me solve problems and act creatively. (Proverbs 8:12)

If you seek good principles, then you will be blessed by them. You will become richer and wiser because you have inner strength that's greater than money. You will receive more than tangible goods, wages, stock options, and retirement benefits. You will be guided by inner character and will do things right. If you love God, then He will have an inheritance for you and will bless your life. If we ignore His principles, then we hurt ourselves because if we hate wisdom, then we love death. (Proverbs 8:16–21, 36)

If you live wisely, then you have plenty of meat to eat and plenty to drink and a table full of delicious desserts and you give good advice to others. (Proverbs 9:2–3)

If you are a wise man, then you will listen to instruction because a wise man wants to learn from others so he can improve himself, his family, and his business. (Proverbs 9:8–9)

If you put the Lord at the center of your life, then you will become holy as you follow His wisdom and principles; you will live longer and enjoy the days given you for His wisdom will make you a better person. (Proverbs 9:10–12)

If you are a foolish busybody and listen to gossip, then you become dumber. (Proverbs 9:13–14)

If you are a wise son, then you will please your father, but if you are a foolish son, then you will weigh heavily on your mother. (Proverbs 10:1)

If you live right, then you have the peace the world can't enjoy because all the wealth of wickedness can't give inner happiness. (Proverbs 10:2)

If you live right, then the Lord will give you a full life. (Proverbs 10:3)

If you are a lazy man, then you will eventually become poor, but if you are diligent, then you will become prosperous. (Proverbs 10:4)

If you live by right principles, then God will add value to you, but if you rebel against His laws, then you will suffer the consequences of His broken laws. (Proverbs 10:6)

If you live uprightly, then you will have confidence, but if you undermine the steps of others, you will eventually fail at all you do. (Proverbs 10:9)

If you speak the right things, then you will help others, but if you condone breaking His principles, then you will eventually suffer the violence of those broken laws. If you love, then you overlook the faults of others, but if you hate, then you stir up strife. (Proverbs 10:11–12)

If you are wise, then you want to learn more wise things, but if you don't care about learning anything, then you are a fool and are destroying any chance of a good life. (Proverbs 10:14)

If you are a wise man, then you have many kinds of treasures that protect you in many ways, but if you are fool, then you have only your poverty, which cannot protect you from destruction. (Proverbs 10:15)

If you follow His unchanging principles, then you are walking in the way of eternal life. (Proverbs 10:17)

If you are wise, then you are able to discipline your words, but if you are a fool, then you hide your hatred and slander with lies like those who oppose your way of life. (Proverbs 10:18)

If you do right, then your works are worth lots of money, but if you have the heart of an evil man, then they are not worth much. (Proverbs 10:20)

If you do right, then your speech helps many, but if you are a fool, then people die who listen to you. (Proverbs 10:21)

If you are wicked, then you usually experience the thing you fear, but if you desire to do right, then you usually get what you want in life. (Proverbs 10:24)

If you are wicked, then your death comes like a blowing wind and you are gone and nothing remains, but if you do right, then you leave a lasting influence on people when you die. (Proverbs 10:25)

If you do right, then the Lord lengthens your years, but if you are wicked, then your life is shortened. If you do right, then your dreams bring joy, but if you are wicked, then your expectations pass away. (Proverbs 10:27–28)

If you do God's will, then it will give you strength, but if you rebel against God's will, then your strength will be gone. (Proverbs 10:29)

If you do right, then you will know what to say, but if you are evil, then you will never have the right words. If you do right, then you will live forever, but if you do wickedness, then you will not inhabit the earth. (Proverbs 10:30–32)

If I follow Your principles, then I have true self-understanding, but If I am driven by my ego, then I end up embarrassing myself. (Proverbs 11:2)

If I want to know the truth, Lord, then You deliver me, but if I am a liar, then allow me to be destroyed by my lies. If I seek to be righteous, then I will be saved. (Proverbs 11:6, 8)

If the people of a city obey Your laws, then it is blessed, but if they listen to the evil speech of the rebels, then it is overthrown. (Proverbs 11:11)

If you are a faithful friend, then you don't embarrass others, and if you seek wisdom, then you get safe advice. (Proverbs 11:14)

If you are a gracious woman, then you are loved, but if you are hateful, then you will be hated by others. If you are a strong man, then you are respected. If you are merciful, then you get mercy. (Proverbs 11:16–17)

If you are an evil person, then you gain nothing from what you earn, but if you are a good person, you will surely be rewarded. (Proverbs 11:18)

If you are a truly good person, then you will live, but if you are one who chases after evil, then you will die. (Proverbs 11:19)

If you do right, then you are the Lord's delight, but if you lie, then you are an abomination to the Lord. (Proverbs 11:20)

If you are a beautiful woman and act like a fool, then you are like a beautiful jewel in a pig's nose. (Proverbs 11:22)

If you give away goods, then you will eventually get them back, but if you withhold your goods, then you will end up in poverty. (Proverbs 11:23)

If you add value to others, then you will have value added to you. (Proverbs 11:25)

If you diligently seek good, then you will find it, but if you seek evil, then you will be found by it. (Proverbs 11:27)

If you think your money will get you ahead, then you will always fall behind. If you always do the right thing, then you will flourish like a fruitful farm. (Proverbs 11:28)

If you make trouble for the family, then you will inherit the whirlwind. If you are a fool, then you will always be a slave to the wise one who does the right thing. (Proverbs 11:29)

If you do the right thing, then your fruit grows on the tree of the wise, and if you do right, you will be rewarded with right things, but if you are wicked, then you will be rewarded with wickedness. (Proverbs 11:30–31)

If you are a woman who lives wisely, then you are a crown to your husband, but if you are a woman who embarrasses her husband, then you are like a cancer in the bones. (Proverbs 12:4)

If you think about doing right, then you will do right, but if you listen to wicked counsel, then you will deceive yourself. If you are wicked, then you will always fail and your name will be forgotten. (Proverbs 12:5, 7)

If you plow and plant your ground, then you will have bread to eat after harvest, but if you're a lazy man, then you won't do anything and will not have food to eat. (Proverbs 12:11)

If you are a fool, you think you always do the right thing, but if you're a wise person, then you listen to wise counsel and get ahead. (Proverbs 12:15)

If you're a fool, then your words pierce like a knife, but if you are wise, then your counsel gives health. (Proverbs 12:18)

If you're a fool, then you deceive people because you continually plan evil, but if you listen to truth, then you will always be happy. If you are a fool, then you always talk about foolish things, but if you are wise, then you think about what is right. (Proverbs 12:23)

If you always speak good words, then it will make your life easier and happy, but if you speak discouraging words, then it will make an old person out of you. (Proverbs 12:25)

If you live continually by the right principles, then you are a testimony to your neighbors, but if you are a lazy man, then you try to get everyone to live at your level of incompetence and activity. If you are lazy, then you won't take advantage of opportunities, but if you're diligent, then you will turn them into money. (Proverbs 12:26–27)

If you do right, then you follow the path of eternal life, but if you are a procrastinator, then you will be on the path that leads to death. (Proverbs 12:28)

If you speak good words, then you will prosper, but if you're a rebel, then you will eventually get violence. (Proverbs 13:2)

If I control my speech, then I will properly discipline my life; but if I don't care what I say, then I will be destroyed. (Proverbs 13:3)

If I work diligently, then I will prosper, but if I am lazy, then I have nothing even though I want everything. (Proverbs 13:4)

If I live right and speak the truth, then I will not be wicked and eventually get caught in my lies. (Proverbs 13:5)

If I have right thinking, then it will keep me doing right things, but if I am wicked and have evil desires, then it will always trip me up. (Proverbs 13:6)

If I live right, then I will enjoy the life you have given me, but if I am wicked, then I will be tripped up by my wicked thoughts. (Proverbs 13:8)

If I learn to live right by listening to wise people, then I won't be proud and get irritated with them. If I work diligently, then I will increase my bank account; but if I am arrogant, then I will lose money for not taking advice. (Proverbs 13:10)

If despise your Word, then I will be destroyed, but if I live by Your principles, then I will be rewarded. (Proverbs 13:13)

If I have right thinking, then I will focus on others, but if I break the law, then I will have a hard time. (Proverbs 13:15)

If I learn from the counsel of the wise, then I will not reject correction and be embarrassed by my failure and poverty. (Proverbs 13:18)

If I make friends with people who think right, then they will influence me to live right; but if I have friends who are fools, then I will suffer the same consequences as fools. (Proverbs 13:20)

If I live right, then I will be rewarded by righteousness, but if I am a rebel, then I will be chased down and beaten to death. (Proverbs 13:21)

If I am a good person, then my inheritance will extend to my grandchildren, but if I am evil, then the inheritance will go to those who live right. (Proverbs 13:22)

If I correct my children, then their decision-making won't be corrupted and I demonstrate my love to them by making them do right. (Proverbs 13:24)

If I live right, then I will have a satisfying life, but if I live evil, then my desires are never satisfied. (Proverbs 13:25)

If I am a wise woman, then I will strengthen my family, but if I am a foolish woman, then I will tear it down with foolish actions. (Proverbs 14:1)

If I search for Your wisdom, Lord, then it's easy to find it. (Proverbs 14:6)

If I am wise, then I will avoid danger, but if I am a fool, then I will walk recklessly too close to the edge and become quick-tempered, make bad decisions, and be hated for my sinful acts and my stupidity. (Proverbs 14:16)

If I plan to do good, then You, Lord, give me grace, but if I do evil, then I will go astray. (Proverbs 14:22)

If I work hard, then I will get ahead, but if I only talk, then I will get nothing. (Proverbs 14:23)

If I work hard, I will be rewarded, but if I am a fool, then I will be rewarded with foolishness. (Proverbs 4:24)

If I tell the truth, then I will help others, but if I am a liar, then I am a traitor to everyone I speak to. (Proverbs 14:25)

If I fear You, Lord, then I am secure, my children enjoy Your refuge, I drink the goodness of life from Your fountain and escape the temptations that lead to death. (Proverbs 14:26–27)

If I am a wise leader, then I will attract many followers, but if I have a lesser group following me, then it shows my influence is declining. (Proverbs 14:28)

If I control my anger, then I am very wise, but if I have a quick temper, then I make foolish mistakes. (Proverbs 14:29)

If I keep a tranquil spirit, then I'll be healthy, but if I envy and hate, then I will rot away. (Proverbs 14:30)

If I have mercy on the needy, then I will honor You, Lord, but if I oppress the poor, then I insult You. (Proverbs 14:31)

If I give a soft answer, then it will turn away wrath, but if I use angry words, then it will stir up anger. If I use wisely all I've learned, then I will not be like the fool who spouts foolishness. (Proverbs 15:1–2)

If I am righteous, then You will delight in my prayers, but if I am wicked, then You reject my good works. (Proverbs 15:8)

If my heart rejoices, then I have a happy face, but if I am a scorner, then it breaks the human spirit. (Proverbs 15:13)

If I get the help of a good counselor, then I will make good plans, but without wise advice, then my plans will go awry. (Proverbs 15:22)

If I say the right thing at the right time, then people will listen to a fitting reply. (Proverbs 15:23)

If I follow the path that leads to life above, then I will avoid the rebellious ways that lead to hell. (Proverbs 15:24)

If I am arrogant and think I've made it by myself, then the Lord will destroy my things, but protect the property of widows. (Proverbs 15:25)

If I am right acting, then You hear my prayers, but if I am wicked, then You shut Your ears. (Proverbs 15:29)

If I listen to the wise, then I will grow in understanding, but if I don't listen to others, then I will hurt myself. (Proverbs 15:32)

If I commit myself to think right, Lord, then my actions will be successful. (Proverbs 16:3)

If I think I am better than others, then that is an abomination; that attitude will not escape punishment. (Proverbs 16:5)

If my actions please You, Lord, then my enemies cannot accuse me of anything. (Proverbs 16:7)

If I have pride, then it will trip me up in many ways. If I have a rebellious spirit, then it will destroy me. (Proverbs 16:18)

If I choose to think right and be wise, then it will show when I speak. (Proverbs 16:23)

If I speak good words, then I will have a happy life and they will give life to the whole body. (Proverbs 16:24)

If each person thinks he chooses the right path without You, Lord, then the path leads to death. (Proverbs 16:25)

If you are a sinner thirsting for more sin, then your lips are burned when you drink it. (Proverbs 16:27)

If you want to glorify the Lord in your old age, then always think right to live successfully. (Proverbs 16:31)

If I keep my temper, then I will be mightier than the mighty. If I conquer my inner spirit, then I will be like those who conquer a city. (Proverbs 16:32)

If you mock the poor, then you make fun of the Lord who made all people. If you rejoice at the accident of others, then you will suffer accidents. (Proverbs 17:5)

If I give a gift in good faith, then I will get good will when I give a gift. (Proverbs 17:8)

If I overlook others' faults, then my love for them is strengthened. If I point out others' problems, then it separates the best of friends. (Proverbs 17:9)

If you break rules, then you are rebellious in your heart and will only learn from the cruel consequences of your mistakes. (Proverbs 17:11)

If people give evil to people who do them good, then they will have more evil than they can bear; they will never get rid of evil. (Proverbs 17:13)

If I guarantee a loan for someone, then I am responsible for his debts. If you enjoy arguing, then you also enjoy sinning. If you brag about your strengths, then you invite attacks. (Proverbs 17:18)

If you have twisted ideas, then you do not try to live right and if you have a twisted tongue, then you will end up in trouble. (Proverbs 17:20)

If you are a foolish child, then you won't listen to right thinking, which angers a good father and embitters the mother who gave him birth. (Proverbs 17:25)

If you use your knowledge to discipline your speech, then you are a wise person who can control your temper. (Proverbs 17:27)

If you are a recluse or a hermit, then you selfishly think only of yourself and deny every principle of getting along with people. (Proverbs 18:1)

If you are a fool, then you never try to learn from others and only want to arrogantly express your advice. If you are a wicked person, then you bring rebellion and disrespect into the room and arguments follow. (Proverbs 18:2–3)

If the mouth of a fool keeps him in trouble, then he can't do right because his words continually trip him up. (Proverbs 18:7)

If you gossip, which is slippery sweet like honey, then it'll slip into the belly and make you sick. (Proverbs 18:8)

If you are a lazy man who never accomplishes anything, then you are as bad as one who destroys what others accomplish. (Proverbs 18:9)

If I think right, then I can make it through sickness, but if my spirit is deflated, then I give up. (Proverbs 8:14)

If you offend a brother, then it's harder to win back the friendship than to win a big physical fight because the offense is taken to heart. (Proverbs 18:19)

If you have good food in your mouth, then it satisfies the belly just like good words make the spirit happy. (Proverbs 18:20)

If you find a good wife, then you discover the greatest treasure to possess and you get the Lord's blessing in life. (Proverbs 18:22)

If you are friendly, then you will have friends and the Lord is the friend who is closer than a brother. (Proverbs 18:24)

If you lie, then it will always add grief to the liar; you will not escape your punishment. (Proverbs 19:5)

IF? THEN!

If you have right thinking, then you will prosper. If you put up a false front, then you will be embarrassed, and if you tell lies, then you will be punished. (Proverbs 19:8

If I discipline my anger, then I will be wise and overlook the mistakes of others. (Proverbs 19:11)

If you are a foolish son, then you will disappoint your father, and if you are a nagging wife, then you irritate your husband like a faucet that keeps dripping. (Proverbs 19:13)

If you are a lazy person who sleeps instead of working, then you will go hungry. (Proverbs 19:15

If I live correctly, Lord, then I will obey Your commands, but if I despise Your way of life, then I will die. (Proverbs 19:16)

If I help the poor, then I am lending You, Lord, who will repay me in many ways. (Proverbs 19:17)

If I discipline my children while they can learn, then their lives won't be ruined. (Proverbs 19:18)

If I am a violent-tempered person, then I will pay for my anger. (Proverbs 19:19)

If I obey good advice and learn from discipline, then I'll have a good life for the rest of my life. (Proverbs 19:20)

If I reverently trust You for eternal life, then evil will not be able to touch me. (Proverbs 19:23)

If children mistreat their father or reject their mother, then they are a disgrace and embarrassment to them. (Proverbs 19:26)

If I stop listening to correction, then I have turned my back on common sense. (Proverbs 19:27)

If you are a lying witness, then you make a mockery of justice and wicked people drink in evil. (Proverbs 19:28)

If you are a scorner, then you will be judged for your scorn just as surely as fools will be judged. (Proverbs 19:29)

If wine makes a mockery of wise people, and liquor leads to fights, then I will not be led astray by using it. (Proverbs 20:1)

If any fool can fly off the handle in rage, then I will become wise by avoiding quarrels. (Proverbs 20:3)

If you are too lazy to plow, then in the spring you won't have any food in the harvest. (Proverbs 20:4)

If I think right and walk in integrity, then my children may happily follow my example. (Proverbs 20:7)

If I want to be innocent and transparent like a child, then everyone will know the purity of my heart. (Proverbs 20:11)

If I will not spend my days sleeping but rather open my eyes to the tasks before me, then my needs will be supplied. (Proverbs 20:13)

If I steal or lie to get something illegally, then it will turn sour in my stomach. (Proverbs 20:17)

If I seek advice when attempting something big, then I will make good plans to have success in life. (Proverbs 20:18)

If you curse your father and mother, then your lamp will be put out and you'll be in darkness. (Proverbs 20:20)

If I get a belonging too soon and too easily, then I usually don't appreciate it in the long run. (Proverbs 20:21)

If I pledge money to You and then change my mind and not give it, then it is a sin. (Proverbs 20:25)

If you have haughty eyes and an arrogant attitude, then they are just as much a sin as all the actions that break Your law. (Proverbs 21:4)

If I have good planning and work hard, then I will succeed, but if I goof off and give it my second best, then I will fail. (Proverbs 21:5)

If wealth is accumulated by lying, then it will vanish like the early fog because it is a sedative trap that leads to death. (Proverbs 21:6)

If you shut your ears to the requests of the poor, then you will be ignored when your time of need comes. (Proverbs 21:13)

If you stray from the path of common sense, then you will end up dead like others who violated God's law. (Proverbs 21:16)

If you are given to pleasure, then you will end up poor; and if you are given to wine, then you will never succeed. (Proverbs 21:17)

When I seek to think right and live right, then You promise me life, wisdom, and honor. (Proverbs 21:21)

If I discipline my thinking and words, then I will stay out of trouble. (Proverbs 21:23)

If you are too lazy to work for the things you want, then the craving of being a lazy man will eat you up. (Proverbs 21:25)

If you are a lying witness, then you will eventually be punished, but if you know the truth, then you will be allowed to speak. (Proverbs 21:28)

If you are a wise man, then you see problems coming and get out of the way, but if you are naive, then problems will run over you and you will suffer the consequences. (Proverbs 22:3)

If I fear You, then I have a proper view of myself and I will be properly equipped to make money. (Proverbs 22:4)

If you are stubborn, then you will run into a lot of difficulties, but if you believe right, then you will be able to avoid them. (Proverbs 22:5)

If I properly train a child to believe and act right, then he will live right when he grows up. (Proverbs 22:6)

If you have a generous spirit, then you add value to your life because you share with the needy. (Proverbs 22:9)

If you are conscientious and give compliments, then you will get the attention of the boss. (Proverbs 22:11)

If I pay attention when the wise instruct me, then I can gain knowledge and wisdom. (Proverbs 22:17)

If I have the principles of wise people in my heart, then I can explain why I live by God's rules. (Proverbs 22:18)

If I put my trust in the Lord alone, then I can tell others how to live for God. (Proverbs 22:19)

If I associate with angry people and become close friends with those who lose their temper easily, then being around them will make me become like them, and I'll suffer the consequences of their mean-spiritedness. (Proverbs 22:24)

If I gorge my stomach with food, then I will embarrass myself. (Proverbs 23:2)

If I lust after delicacies and am greedy for dainties, then it reveals my lack of character and is not healthy and nourishing. (Proverbs 23:3)

If I am wise enough to control myself, then I will not exhaust myself pursuing money. If I set my eyes on riches, then I'll lose sight of everything else in life. (Proverbs 23:4)

If I want my children to learn wisdom, then I'll be glad when they speak wise words.
(Proverbs 23:15)

If I follow the example of those who follow You, then I'll not be cut down in the prime of life because a solid future is with those who fear You. (Proverbs 23:18)

If we can't say NO to liquor or beer, then we will continually search for a mixed drink and if we look with desire into the glass as it gives off its smell and smooth color that slides smoothly down the throat and seems like a heavenly taste, then the liquor bites like a striking serpent. Its sip is the venom of a deadly snake, so I determine never to take my first drink. (Proverbs 23:30–32)

If I am wise, then I can be strong and increase my strength with knowledge. (Proverbs 24:5)

If I know that I should get wisdom because it is good for me and its taste is sweet to the desires of the soul, then when I get it, wisdom will give me what I hope for. (Proverbs 24:14)

If I give an honest answer to those who ask, then it's like giving a kiss to those you respect. (Proverbs 24:26)

If I have told publicly what was told to me privately, then I'll be embarrassed and my reputation will be ruined. (Proverbs 25:10)

If you give false testimony against a neighbor, then that will hurt them like a club, a sharp sword, or a piercing arrow. (Proverbs 25:18)

If I rely on an untrustworthy person in a time of trouble, then it is like having a toothache or a crippled leg. (Proverbs 25:19)

If we sing sad songs to people in trouble, then it is like taking away their coat in cold weather. (Proverbs 25:20)

If someone who hates me is hungry, I'll give him food, for then I'll heap hot coals on his head and You, Lord, will reward me. (Proverbs 25:21)

If I eat too much honey or try to seek my own glory, then both excesses will make me sick. (Proverbs 25:27)

If a person gives a curse to someone who doesn't deserve it, then that person will be punished with that curse. (Proverbs 26:2)

If a whip will make a donkey obey, then correcting is the only way to help a fool. (Proverbs 26:3)

If I answer a fool according to his foolishness, then I'll lower myself to his disgusting level. (Proverbs 26:4)

If I answer a fool according to truth, then he'll know he is not wise. (Proverbs 26:5)

If you let a fool deliver a message for you, then that is like asking for trouble and pain. (Proverbs 26:6)

If you try to give honor to a fool, then it is like trying to shoot a gun without bullets. (Proverbs 26:8)

If you are a master craftsman, then you can make a work of art, but if you employ a fool, then it is like breaking the laws of common sense. (Proverbs 26:10)

If you are a lazy person, then you have more excuses for what you do than the reasons of seven wise men. (Proverbs 26:16)

If I get involved in a fight that's not my own, then it's like grabbing a dog by its ears; I'll get bitten. (Proverbs 26:17)

If there is no wood, then the fire goes out; if gossip stops, then so does contention. (Proverbs 26:20)

If coals are to start a fire and burning wood makes heat, then so does a quarreling person cause strife. (Proverbs 26:21)

If the lies of a slanderer are easily swallowed, then they make everyone else sick to their stomachs. (Proverbs 26:22)

If those who hate try to cover it with pleasant words, then they can't eliminate their deceitful heart. (Proverbs 26:24)

If you dig a pit, then you will eventually fall into it and what goes around comes around and you will eventually suffer the evil you planned for others. (Proverbs 26:27)

If you tell lies, then you will eventually hate your victims and a flattering tongue is a sugar-coated lie, so I will tell the truth because I love you, Lord, and others. (Proverbs 26:28)

If I am full, then I have no taste for honey; but if I'm hungry, then anything bitter tastes sweet. (Proverbs 27:7)

If a man foolishly strays from his home, then he is like a bird that abandons its protective nest. (Proverbs 27:8)

If perfume and sweet-smelling things makes us happy, then so does good advice from the heart of a friend. (Proverbs 27:9)

If I become wise to make my father glad, then I won't need my father to answer my critics. (Proverbs 27:11)

If I want to be wise to avoid trouble when it comes, then I won't be a fool who doesn't think about the future and pays the price. (Proverbs 27:12)

If you are a nagging wife that keeps at it, then you are like dripping water on a rainy day that will only irritate and anger. (Proverbs 27:15)

If you carefully look after the fig tree, then you get to enjoy its fruit, and if you do what the boss wants you to do, then you will be honored and promoted. (Proverbs 27:18)

If I can see my image reflected in water, then so others can see my heart by looking at my face. (Proverbs 27:19)

If I let greed motivate my heart to get what it sees, then like hell and the grave, they are never satisfied. (Proverbs 27:20)

If you get rich by charging too much, then you create wealth for someone else to give to the poor. (Proverbs 28:8)

If you refuse to obey God's principles, then you will not get your prayers answered. (Proverbs 28:9)

If you tempt the righteous to break God's law, then you will suffer the punishment God plans for them. (Proverbs 28:10)

If the good man wins, then everyone rejoices, but no one wants to see a wicked man win. (Proverbs 28:12)

If you hide your sin, then you will not get away with it, but God will accept those who confess and repent. (Proverbs 28:13)

If you fear and obey God, then you are happy, but if you harden your heart, then you will have a hard life. (Proverbs 28:14)

If you are a rising leader without wisdom, then you are a cruel oppressor, but if you are a leader who hates greed, then you will stay in office. (Proverbs 28:16)

If you kill another, then you deserve to die. (Proverbs 28:17)

If you obey God's principles, then you will be saved, but if you reject God's ways, then you will not live long. (Proverbs 28:18)

If you work hard at your job, then you will have food to eat, but if you frolic with lazy people, then you will be poor. (Proverbs 28:19)

If you are a trustworthy worker, then you will receive bonuses and raises, but if you cut corners, then you will be demoted or fired. (Proverbs 28:20)

If you are a greedy person who will sell his soul for money, then not knowing your insatiable appetite will ultimately choke you to death, but if you are a starving man, then you will steal for bread. (Proverbs 28:22)

If I correct my brother to help him, then I'll get more gratitude than if I flatter his sin and disobedience. (Proverbs 28:23)

If you steal from your parents because you think you deserve it because you are their child, then you are brothers to Satan. (Proverbs 28:24)

If you grasp after attention, then you create strife and anger in those around you, but if you obey God's principles, then you will prosper and get the right kind of attention. (Proverbs 28:25)

If you trust in yourself, then you are a fool, but if you live right, then you will prosper. (Proverbs 28:26)

If you give to the poor, then you will not lack anything, but if you turn your back on the poor, then you will be cursed by them. (Proverbs 28:27)

If I harden my neck after being rebuked, then I will be suddenly broken. (Proverbs 29:1)

If the righteous are our leaders, then everyone rejoices because the leaders do right. If the wicked are over us, then everyone moans because evil flourishes. (Proverbs 29:2)

If I seek to think the right way, then I make my father glad; but if I visit a prostitute, then I waste my money and my life. (Proverbs 29:3)

If rulers do right, then they give us a stable nation, but if the rulers take bribes, then they destroy the people. (Proverbs 29:4)

If you try to get ahead by flattery, then you spread a trap for your own feet. (Proverbs 29:5)

If an evil man commits crimes, then it will eventually catch him, but if the righteous have a clean conscience, then they can sing and dance. (Proverbs 29:6)

If you are a negative critic, then you make everyone mad, but if you are wise, then your words have a calming effect. (Proverbs 29:8)

If a wise man argues with a fool, then he only gets scorn and ridicule, and angry replies. (Proverbs 29:9)

If you want to kill, then you hate those who obey God's principles and will attempt to do away with them. (Proverbs 29:10)

If you are a fool, then you rattle on about everything you don't like, but if you are a wise person, then you hold your tongue and think through the situation. (Proverbs 29:11)

If you are a leader who listens and believes lies, then you have counselors around you who are wicked. (Proverbs 29:12)

If a leader trusts the poor with honesty, then he will be in office a long time.
(Proverbs 29:14)

If you leave a child to himself without correction, then the child will disgrace his parents. (Proverbs 29:15)

If the wicked rule, then more people will break the rules. (Proverbs 29:16)

If you discipline your child, then he will make you happy; he will do what you expect him to do. (Proverbs 29:17)

If I don't have divine direction in my life, then I'll shrivel up spiritually, but I'll be happy if I obey Your law. (Proverbs 29:18)

If you have something to say about everything, then you have as much hope as a fool. (Proverbs 29:20)

If you pamper a child from his youth, then he will be ungrateful when he grows up.
(Proverbs 29:21)

If you are an angry person, then you stir up strife and bitterness and if you have an uncontrollable temper, then you commit crimes. (Proverbs 29:22)

If I am proud, then I will be brought low, but if I humble myself, then I will be honored. (Proverbs 29:23)

If you partner with a thief, then you hate your-self. (Proverbs 29:2)

If you are afraid of others, then they can trap you, but if you put your trust in the Lord, then you will be safe. (Proverbs 29:25)

If you are a wicked man, then you are always against the righteous person because you detest them. (Proverbs 29:27)

If you are more boorish than others, then you are too ignorant to seek to understand God. (Proverbs 30:2)

If you take refuge in the Lord, then He will pro-tect you because every word He speaks is pure. (Proverbs 30:5)

If I add anything to Your words, then You will rebuke me and I'll be made to be a liar. (Proverbs 30:6)

If I have too much money, then I may deny You and say, "Who is the Lord?" If I am poor, then I might steal and tarnish Your name. (Proverbs 30:9)

If I ever criticize a person to his employer, then he will slander me for my interference. (Proverbs 30:10)

If you justify your actions and think you never do anything wrong, then you are haughty and stupid. (Proverbs 30:12)

If your eye mocks your father and criticizes the requests of your mother, then your eyes will be pecked out by the birds, and you'll be judged for your rebellion. (Proverbs 30:17)

If I seek pleasure in strong drink and taste liquor, then drinking will distort my understanding of Your law and drunkenness will make me forget my duties and will not give happiness; it brings misery and if I am given to strong drink, then I will be destroyed. (Proverbs 31:4–6)

Book of Zechariah

If you return to Me, then I will return to you.
(Zechariah 1:3)

Book of Malachi

If you bring the entire 10 percent into the temple storehouse so there will be enough food there, then I'll open the windows of heaven and pour blessing after blessing on you. (Malachi 3:10)

If you reverence My name, then righteousness will be as prevalent as the sun, and you'll be free, jumping around like calves let out to pasture. Then you'll tread on the wicked like they're ashes under your feet, says the Lord of the Heavens. (Malachi 4:2–3)

Book of Mark

If you blaspheme the Holy Spirit, then you will never be forgiven and are in danger of eternal damnation. (Mark 3:29)

If you do the will of God, then you are His brothers and sisters and mother. (Mark 3:35)

If you have good ears, then hear and obey. (Mark 4:23)

If you have, then you shall be given more; if you do not have, then you shall lose what you have. (Mark 4:25)

If you become My disciple, then you must say, no to self-interest; take up your cross, and follow Me continually. If you try to save your life, then you will lose it, if you give up your life for Me and the gospel, then you will save it. (Mark 8:34–35)

If you are ashamed of Me and My words in this adulterous sinful age, then the Son of Man shall be ashamed of you when He comes in the Father's glory with the holy angels. (Mark 8:38)

If anyone desires to be the first, then he must be the last and the servant of all. (Mark 9:35)

If you receive Me, then you receive the One who sent Me. (Mark 9:37)

If you are not against Me, then you are for me. (Mark 9:40)

If you give a cup of water in My name I truly say, then you will get your reward. (Mark 9:41)

If you lead one of these children to do wrong, then you might as well have a huge millstone hung around your neck and be thrown into the sea. (Mark 9:42)

If your hand makes you do wrong, then you cut if off. If your foot makes you do wrong, then cut if off. If your eye makes you do wrong, cut it out. (Mark 9:43, 45–47)

If he divorces his wife and marries another, then he commits adultery against her; if she divorces her husband and marries another, then she commits adultery. (Mark 10:11–12)

If you do not receive the kingdom of God as a little child, then you shall not enter into it. (Mark 10:15)

If you will say to a mountain, "Be removed and thrown into the sea" and you don't doubt, but believe that you will receive what you ask, then you shall have it. (Mark 11:23)

If you believe before you pray, then you shall have all things for which you ask. (Mark 11:24)

If you begin to pray, you must forgive those with whom you have an issue so that your Father may forgive your sin; then you have a basis for getting an answer to your prayer. If you do not forgive others, then neither will your heavenly Father forgive your trespasses. (Mark 11:25–26)

If you hear about wars and rumors of war, then don't be alarmed because wars will come, but the end is not yet. (Mark 13:7)

If they try you in court, then you don't have to be concerned about what you should say for it is not you who will be speaking, but the Holy Spirit will speak through you. (Mark 13:11)

If you endure to the end, then you will be saved. (Mark 13:13)

If the Lord does not cut short those days, then no one will escape, but for the sake of the elect, God will cut them short. (Mark 13:20)

If anyone tells you, "Look, the Christ is here! Or, Look, He is there!" then don't believe it for false Christs and false prophets will come and perform signs and wonders to lead you astray; even, if possible, they will lead the elect astray. Watch out. I am warning you before it comes. (Mark 13:21–23)

If He comes unexpectedly, then He might find you sleeping. Watch for His coming! (Mark 13:36)

Book of Luke

If a man strikes you on one cheek, then offer him the other; and if a man takes away your coat, then offer him your shirt also. (Luke 6:29)

If you love only those who love you, then what credit do you get for that? Even big sinners love those who love them. (Luke 6:32)

If you do good only to those who do good to you, then what credit is that? Even big sinners do that. (Luke 6:33)

If you lend to people expecting to get it back, then what credit is that? Even big sinners lend to one another, expecting to get back a full payment. (Luke 6:34)

If you practice loving your enemies, then your reward will be great, and you will be sons of the Most High. (Luke 6:35)

If you stop criticizing others, then you won't be criticized. If you stop judging others, then you will not be judged. If you forgive others, then you will be forgiven. (Luke 6:37)

If you give to others, then you will receive good measure, pressed down, shaken together, and running over and poured into your lap. For the measuring cup you use with others will be used with you. (Luke 6:38)

If you look for a tiny speck in your brother's eye when there is a heavy timber in your own eye, then you must first get the timber out of your own eye, and then you may get the speck out of your brother's eye. (Luke 6:42)

If you are a good man, then your good character bears good fruit. If you are a bad man, then your bad character will bear bad fruit. (Luke 6:43)

If everyone who follows Me and does the things I teach, they will be like a man who is building a house. He digs deep and lays a foundation on bedrock, and when the floods come to burst on that house, then it will stand because it was built on a rock. (Luke 6:47)

If you are a man who merely hears My words, and does not do them, then you are like a man who builds on a house of sand, and when the floods burst upon it, then it will collapse because it has no foundation. (Luke 6:49)

If you take care and believe, then whoever receives more will have more given to him; and whoever does not receive more will even have that taken away from him. (Luke 8:18)

If you hang onto this earthly life for Me, then you will lose it. And anyone who loses his life for My sake, then he will save it. (Luke 9:24)

If you welcome a little child in Jesus' name, then you welcome Me; and if you welcome Me, then you welcome the One who sent Me. (Luke 9:48)

If you put your hand to the plow and look back, then you are not fit for the kingdom of God. (Luke 9:62)

If you love the Lord your God with all your heart, soul, strength, and might, and love your neighbor as yourself, then you will live. (Luke 10:27–28)

If you keep on asking, then you shall receive, keep on seeking, then you will find, keep on knocking, then the door will open. (Luke 11:9)

If fallen people like yourself give good gifts to your children, then how much more will your heavenly Father give you good gifts? (Luke 11:13)

If your eye is healthy, then your whole body has light. But if your eye is diseased, your body can't see to walk. If your whole body is filled with light, then you can walk confidently because the lamp shines on you with its rays. (Luke 11:34, 36)

If you declare yourself for Jesus in the presence of people, then the Son of Man will acknowledge you in the presence of God's angels. If you disown Jesus in the presence of men, then you will be disowned in the presence of God's angels. (Luke 12:8–9)

If you speak a word against the Son of Man, then you will be forgiven, but if you blaspheme the Holy Spirit, then you will not be forgiven. (Luke 12:10)

If God wonderfully dresses the fields with wild grass, which today is green but tomorrow is thrown into the furnace, then how much more will He clothe you who have so little faith? (Luke 12:28)

If you try to honor yourself, then you will be humbled, and if you will humble yourself, then you will be honored. (Luke 14:11)

II you follow Jesus, then you must love Him more than you love your father, mother, sister or brothers, even your own life. (Luke 14:26)

If you are not honest in small things, then you won't be honest in larger matters. (Luke 16:10)

If you have not been faithful in handling the money of others, then you will not be entrusted with your own. (Luke 16:11)

If you are unfaithful in handling worldly wealth, then who would trust you with the eternal wealth of heaven? (Luke 16:12)

No one can love two masters: if you love the first, then you will hate the second, or you will love the second and hate the first. You cannot serve God and money. (Luke 16:13)

If he sins seven times in a day, then you must forgive him each time he repents. (Luke 17:4)

If anyone hold on to things of this life, then he will lose his life and if he gives up his life for Me, then will save his life. (Luke 17:33)

If you do not accept the kingdom of God as a little child, then you will not enter it. (Luke 18:17)

If you have left housing, brothers, sisters, father, mother, children, or land for My sake, then you will receive 100 times more when you receive eternal life. (Luke 18:29)

If you stand firm, then you will establish your souls. (Luke 21:19)

Book of John

If you continually do evil things, then you hate the light and reject it because it exposes their motives and actions. (John 3:20)

If you believe the truth and come to the light, then you will be saved. Their deeds verify their faith that they are of God. (John 3:21)

If you believe in Jesus, then you have discovered the truth of God that has come from heaven. (John 3:33)

If you believe in the Son, then you already have eternal life; and if you have not believed in the Son, then you do not have eternal life, but the punishment of God rests on you. (John 3:36)

If you drink of the water that Jesus gives, then you will never be thirsty again because the water He gives will be an artesian well inside you that gushes up into eternal life. (John 4:14)

If you don't honor the Son, then you don't honor the Father. (John 5:23)

If you receive My Word, and believe in Me, then you have eternal life and will not be judged for your sins, but pass from death unto eternal life. (John 5:24)

If you are in the grave, then the time is coming when all in their graves will hear My voice and be raised. (John 5:28)

If you have obeyed the Father, then you will be raised to the resurrection of life. If you have disobeyed the Father, then you will be raised to the resurrection of the damned. (John 5:29)

If you come to Jesus, the Bread of Life, then you will never hunger. (John 6:35)

If you believe in the Father, then you will have eternal life because this is the will of the Father. (John 6:40)

If you eat from Jesus, who is the Bread of Life which comes from heaven, then you may eat it and not die. If you eat of My bread, then you will live forever. (John 6:48, 50)

If you are thirsty, then come to Me for satisfaction. (John 7:37)

If you believe in Me, then you will have living water flowing out of your inner being. (John 7:38)

If you have not committed a sin, then you may cast the first stone. (John 8:7)

If you abide in My words, then you are truly My disciples. And you'll know the truth, and the truth will set you free. (John 8:31)

If you commit sin, then you are a bond slave to sin. (John 8:34)

If the Son shall make you free, then you shall be truly free. (John 8:36)

If you were of God, then you would listen to My words, but you don't understand them because you are not God. (John 8:37)

If you will obey My words, then you shall never taste death. (John 8:51)

If you are My sheep, then you know My voice and obey me; I know them and they know Me and follow Me. (John 10:27)

If you love your life, then you will lose it and if you don't live for this life, then you will exchange it for eternal life. (John 12:25)

If anyone wants to be My disciple, then they must follow Me. They will be where I am and the Father will honor them when they follow Me. (John 12:26)

If you believe in Me, then you also believe in the Father who sent Me. (John 12:44)

If you believe in Me as a light to all people, then you who believe in Me will not live in darkness. (John 12:46)

If anyone hears and understands My teachings, but rejects them, then I will not judge them for I came to save all people. But if you do not accept My teachings and reject Me, then you will be judged in the last day by what I've said. The Father will judge him because the Father who sent Me told Me what to say, and His words give life eternal. Therefore, everything I am saying comes from the Father in heaven. (John 12:47–50)

If your Lord and Master have washed your feet, then you ought to be willing to wash one another's feet. (John 13:14)

If you know that a servant is not greater than the one who sent him, then happy are you if you know them. (John 13:16–17)

If you believe in Me, then you shall do the works that I do, and even greater ones, because I am going to the Father. (John 14:12)

If you pray and ask in My name, then I'll do it so the Father will be glorified in Me. If you pray for anything in My name, then I will do it. (John 14:12:14)

If you love Me, then obey my commands, and I will ask the Father to send you another person in My place. He will live with you forever. This other Person is the Holy Spirit, the third Person of the Trinity. (John 14:15–17)

If you are unsaved, then you cannot receive Him because you do not believe in Him or know anything about Him. (John 14:17)

If you believe in Me, then you will know the Holy Spirit and He will dwell with you and be in you. (John 14:17)

If you have My commands and keep them then you are the ones who love Me, and those who love Me will be loved by the Father, and I will love them and I'll show Myself to them. (John 14:21)

If you love Me, then you will obey My commands, and My Father will love you and come to live in you. If you don't obey My commands, then you don't love Me. It's not just My Word you reject, it's the Father's Word. (John 14:23–24)

If I live by Your words, then I am a healthy plant because You are the true Vine and my Father is the Gardner. I will abide in You as You abide in me. (John 15:3–4)

If I remain attached to You, then You abide in me and I will bear plenty of fruit because You are the Vine and I am the branch. (John 15:5)

If you will not remain attached to Me, then you will be punished. You'll be like dead branches that are collected and thrown into a fire to be burned. (John 15:6)

If I remain settled in You, Jesus and Your words remain in me, then I can ask what I want and You'll give it to me. (John 15:7)

If you obey His commands, then you are His friend. (John 15:14)

If I ask you anything Father in Jesus' name, then You'll gladly give it to me, because You chose me and challenged me to bear fruit. (John 15:16)

If You hadn't given the truth, then the world wouldn't experience the guilt of their sin, but now they have no excuse. (John 15:22)

If You hadn't done miracles among them, then they would have been blinded in their sins. Now they see and hate both You and the Father. (John 15:24)

Book of Acts

If you repent, then your sins will be forgiven, and be baptized every one of you in the name of the Lord Jesus Christ, and you will receive the gift of the Holy Spirit. (Acts 2:38)

If you repent and turn to God, then your sins can be forgiven and then God can send to you times of refreshing that come from the presence of God. (Acts 3:19)

If you trust in Him, then you are free from all guilt because there is forgiveness for sins in this Man, Jesus, who will declare you righteous. (Acts 13:38–39)

If you are a mocker, then you need to be careful and cast your eyes around and be amazed before you perish. (Acts 13:41)

Book of Romans

If you put your personal trust in the gospel then you declare him righteous—fit for heaven. The just shall live by faith. (Romans 1:17)

If people know You exist, but don't acknowledge You and think they are wise, then they are actually foolish. Instead of worshiping You, they worship gods made out of wood, or stones that look like birds, or animals or snakes or corrupt people. (Romans 1:22–23)

If people refuse to acknowledge You, then You give them up to their own irrational and corrupt ideas. (Romans 1:28)

If people criticize others for their sin, then they have no excuse for their personal sin as they do the same sin. In judging others, they condemn themselves because they behave no differently than those they condemn. (Romans 2:1)

If you pass judgment on other people; then you will be judged because you do the same thing. (Romans 2:2)

If you seek God's honor and immortality, then you will earn eternal life from Him. (Romans 2:6)

If some refuse Your truth and do evil, then You will punish them in Your anger and fury. (Romans 2:8)

If you are either Jew or Gentile, then both will suffer pain and suffering because they rebelled against You and chased evil. But there will be glory, honor, and peace to those who seek Your salvation, including both Jews and Gentiles. (Romans 2:9–10)

If all have faith, then all are forgiven; it doesn't make any difference if they are circumcised or uncircumcised. If we realize salvation is by faith alone, then this places the law in its proper place. (Romans 3:30)

If you work, then you earn wages and get what is due you. (Romans 4:4)

If you get salvation free, then you have not worked for it. You are justified by your faith. (Romans 4:5)

If unsaved people can receive Your forgiveness by keeping the law, then our faith is pointless and empty. (Romans 4:14)

If my faith is in Jesus, then I can enter Your grace, and I can boast of looking forward to Your glory. Also, I can rejoice in my sufferings, knowing they work patience in my life, and patience produces endurance. When I endure, I get Your approval, which gives me hope. (Romans 5:2–4)

If Jesus' death reconciled me to you, then I was still not saved; I was still Your enemy. Now that I am reconciled, surely I can count on Your blessings by the life of Your Son living in me. (Romans 5:10)

If I was baptized into Christ, then I died when He died. When Christ was raised from the dead, I was given new life to live for Him. I have been united with Christ in death that I might share His new life. (Romans 6:4–5)

If I am dead to sin, then I am free from all its power over me. (Romans 6:7)

If I give myself to sin, then I become a slave to the one I obey. I cannot be a slave to sin and death, and at the same time be a slave to Christ and life. (Romans 6:16)

If I become a slave to sin, then I will feel no obligation to obey Your will. I got nothing from serving sin, and now I'm ashamed of what I did because those things lead to death. (Romans 6:20–21)

If I serve sin, then I earn the wages of death, but You gave me eternal life through Christ Jesus, my Lord. (Romans 6:23)

If you give yourselves to your sinful nature, then your lustful passions control your bodies so you bear fruit to death. If we die to our lust that once controlled us, then we are released from the law so we can serve You in a new way, not by legalistically obeying rules and traditions, but by the power of a new life. (Romans 7:5–6)

If I act against what I want to do, then that means the law is good. If I rebel against the law, then it is not me who is doing it, but sin that dwells in me. I know that nothing good lives in me; it's my sinful nature that controls my life. (Romans 7:16–18)

If I try not to do wrong things, then I do them anyway, then when I do the things I don't want to do, it is not my true self doing them; sin controls my life. (Romans 7:20)

If you are in Christ Jesus, then there is no condemnation against you. (Romans 8:1)

If you are dominated by your sinful nature, then you have made up your mind to sin, but if you are dominated by the Holy Spirit, then you have made up your mind to do what He desires of you. (Romans 8:5)

If I follow the dictates of my old nature, then it will lead to death. (Romans 8:6)

If I obey only my old nature, then I have made myself Your enemy. Your old nature has never been your friend, and you can never make it obey you. If you please your old nature, then you never please God. (Romans 8:7–8)

If you are interested in spiritual things, then it's because the Holy Spirit lives in your life. If you know you are God's child, then it's because you possess the Holy Spirit. (Romans 8:9)

If I died physically when obeying my old nature, then I'd be doomed to death; but Your Holy Spirit can stop my rebellion by His power that dwells me. Therefore, I will be led by the Spirit of God and I will be Your child. (Romans 8:13–14)

If I am Your child, then I am also an heir, Your heir, and co-heir with Christ. If I suffer as a Christian, then I will also share in His glory in heaven. (Romans 8:17)

If I trust You, then I am looking forward to getting a new body. If you are already in heaven, then you don't need hope because you have already received your reward. (Romans 8:23–24)

If I continue to trust for something I don't yet have, then I wait patiently and confidently for it. (Romans 8:25)

If I don't know how I ought to pray, then the Holy Spirit intercedes for me. He prays for words I can't understand or express. What the Holy Spirit prays for me is in agreement with You, my heavenly Father. (Romans 8:26–27)

If He prays for me, then the things that will happen to me are for my good. (Romans 8:28)

If You predestined me and called me, then because You called me, You also justified me; and those You justified, You will glorify. (Romans 8:30)

If You are for me, then who can be against me? (Romans 8:31)

If You justify me, who can condemn me? Christ Jesus who died for me and was raised stands at Your right hand to intercede for me. (Romans 8:34)

If I go through trials, then I know I will triumph by the power of Christ who loves me, and died for me because I am certain that nothing can separate me from You. Angels can't do it, neither can the satanic power of hell, nor things present, nor things to come. Nothing can separate me from Your love: not height, nor depth, nor any other creature, for I am safe in Christ, Jesus my Lord. (Romans 8:38–39)

If I recognize Jesus as the Messiah, the Son of God, and have received Him by faith, then I am saved. (Romans 9:8)

If people rebel against You, then You have a perfect right to show Your anger at any time against them. You put up with rebels so You can show Your mercy and richness of grace and kindness. (Romans 9:22–23)

If you believe in Him, then you will not stumble and fall. (Romans 9:33)

If you receive Christ as your Savior, then it is the end of your struggle to be righteous by keeping the law. (Romans 10:4)

If you trust Christ to save you, then He is in reach of any who look for Him. (Romans 10:8)

If you want this salvation, then it is as easy as opening one's mouth to call for it, and opening their heart to You. Salvation is obtained by the Word of Faith, which I received when I believed. (Romans 10:9–10)

If you believe in Christ, then the Scriptures promised you will not be disappointed, and that is surely true. (Romans 10:11)

If you call on the Lord, then you shall be saved. (Romans 10:13)

If You recognize the Jews for good works, then Your grace would no longer be free. (Romans 11:15)

If you did not spare the natural branches—the Jews—then You will not spare the Gentiles when they reject You. (Romans 11:21)

If I have Your mercy, then I offer myself as a living sacrifice, holy and pleasing to You; this is the first and best spiritual worship to You. I will not allow myself to be conformed to the principles of this world, but I will let my thinking be transformed by the power of the Holy Spirit. Then I will discover Your will for my life, which will glorify You and satisfy my desires. (Romans 12:1–2)

If I have received grace from You, then I will not exaggerate my value or importance. I will honestly estimate the gifts You've given me by the standards of faith You've given me. (Romans 12:3)

If I love everyone as You loved me, then I will not pretend to love people when I don't; I will seek the good things of life, and I will turn my back on evil things. I will love others as Your children should, and have deep respect for others. (Romans 12:9–10)

If Your saints are in need, then I will share with them the things I have and open my home to them. (Romans 12:13)

If I am persecuted, then I will bless those who persecute me, and I will never curse them. (Romans 12:14)

If your enemy is hungry, then you must give him food, and if your enemy is thirsty, then you must give him water to drink, and thus heap hot coals upon his head. (Romans 12:20)

If I live honestly and correctly, then I won't be afraid of punishment. (Romans 13:3)

If I owe anyone anything, then I will give everyone what I owe them, and if I owe taxes, then I will pay them. (Romans 13:7)

If I'm required to respect officials, then I will respect them and honor them. (Romans 13:7)

If I love others, then I will fulfill my debt. Love is the one act that will not hurt my neighbor and it's the only law I need. (Romans 13:8, 10)

If You help me live as I should, then I will not plan to do anything evil. (Romans 13:14)

If you think it's all right to eat meat, then you should not look down on those who don't. And those who don't eat meat should not find fault with those who do. (Romans 14:3)

If I live, then I live for You and when I die, I go to be with You. Whether I am alive or dead, I belong to You. (Romans 14:8)

If some think certain food is unclean, then it is unclean to them. If my attitude toward food is upsetting other believers, then I will be guided by love and I will not eat anything I choose if that means the downfall of a believer for whom Christ has died. (Romans 14:14–15)

If I serve Christ with a respectful attitude toward both eating or abstaining from food, then I will please You and be respected by others. I will adopt any custom that leads to peace and mutual respect by all believers. (Romans 14:18–19)

If I believe I am a strong Christian, then I have a duty to bear the burdens of weak Christians lest they fall. I will be considerate of others and help them become stronger Christians. (Romans 15:1–2)

If I treat others the same way Christ treated other people, then I will glorify You. (Romans 15:7)

If Your hope gives me such power and peace, then the Holy Spirit will overflow me and remove all barriers that hold me back. (Romans 15:13)

If you have real Christian character and experience, then you can keep each other on the straight and narrow path. (Romans 15:14)

If there is anyone in the church who causes division, then I will be on guard against them and I will avoid them in all possible ways. (Romans 16:17)

Book of 1 Corinthians

If the church wants to live in harmony so the body of Christ won't be ruptured, then they must quit fussing among themselves, and be one unified mind in the church. (1 Corinthians 1:10)

If you chose people whom the world thinks are foolish, then it was to confound those the world considers smart; You chose people without influence and those whom the world calls "low class." You chose people hated by the world to show up those the world thinks are brilliant, so no one can ever boast of their accomplishments or that they had something to do with their salvation. (1 Corinthians 1:27–29)

If anyone wants to boast, then let him boast about what the Lord has done. (1 Corinthians 1:31)

If great men understood Your wisdom, then they would never have crucified the Lord of glory. (1 Corinthians 2:8)

If I understand Your plan for all people, then it is because You sent the Holy Spirit to teach it to me. (1 Corinthians 2:10)

If You have given me the Holy Spirit who is different from the spirit of this world, then it is so I can understand Your gifts and plans for me. (1 Corinthians 2:12)

If you are an average unsaved person, then you can't understand His plans for they sound foolish to you. Nor can the unsaved know what the Holy Spirit is saying for the unsaved are spiritually blind. (1 Corinthians 2:14)

If their good works are burned up, then they will be losers, but if they stand the test, then they will be rewarded. (1 Corinthians 3:13)

If anyone destroys Your temple, then You will destroy them. My body is the temple where You dwell. (1 Corinthians 3:17)

If you think you are wise by worldly standards, then you have fooled yourselves because the world's wisdom is folly in Your sight. (1 Corinthians 3:18–19)

If you are a servant of God, then the most important thing is to be found faithful. (1 Corinthians 4:2)

If you have a clear conscience, then that is not enough to prove you're right; You alone, Lord, will tell us what is right. So I'll not prematurely judge if anyone is good, and I'll leave that until

Christ returns. Then all hidden things will be revealed and we'll know what each of us is like and everyone will get the reward he deserves. (1 Corinthians 4:4–5)

If you are cursed, then, like Paul, bless your attackers and be patient with those who injure you. Like Paul, answer quietly when insulted, even when people treat you like dirt. (1 Corinthians 4:12–13)

If those who claim to be Christians but indulge in sexual sins are sexually immoral, greedy, liars, thieves, and idol worshipers, then you need to disassociate; don't even eat a fellowship meal with them. (1 Corinthians 5:10–11)

If people outside the church commit sin, then it is not the church's task to judge them, but it is the job of believers to hold members of the church accountable when they sin and disgrace Christianity; the believers must put them out of the church. (1 Corinthians 5:12–13)

If a Christian files lawsuits, then it is embarrassing; it means you live defeated lives. You ought to accept injustice and let it go because you are the ones doing wrong and you do an injustice to your fellow believers. (1 Corinthians 6:7–8)

If you are an immoral person, then you have no share in the kingdom of God. This includes: idol worshipers, adulterers, homosexuals, thieves, greedy people, drunkards, slanderers, and swindlers. (1 Corinthians 6:9–10)

If I am a believer, then I can do anything I want, but these things are not good for me. Even if I am allowed to do them, then I will not become an addict to sin. (1 Corinthians 6:12)

If our bodies were not created for sexual sin, then sexual sin is never right. They were created as Your dwelling place, and You, Lord must dwell in the temple of our bodies. (1 Corinthians 6:15)

If You have bought me from sin and You paid for me with the blood of Christ, then I will use my body to glorify You. (1 Corinthians 6:20)

If immoral sex is always a temptation, then each man should have his own wife and each woman should have her own husband. The husband must attend to the sexual needs of his wife, and the wife must do the same for her husband. (1 Corinthians 7:2–3)

If a person cannot discipline himself, then it is better to get married than to suffer. (1 Corinthians 7:9)

If a Christian has an unbelieving wife, and he lives peacefully with her, then she must not send him away. If a Christian wife has an unbelieving husband, then she must not send him away, because the unbelieving husband may become a Christian through the influence of his wife, and the same thing may happen to the unbelieving wife. (1 Corinthians 7:13–14)

If there were no Christian influences from a parent, then perhaps the children would not be saved, but they can be saved by the influence of a believing parent. (1 Corinthians 7:15)

If an unbelieving spouse wants to separate, then the believer is not obligated to the marriage. However, if a member of the marriage is a Christian, then a believing wife may lead her husband to Christ, and the Christian husband may lead his unbelieving wife to salvation. (1 Corinthians 7:15–16)

If anyone was uncircumcised when he was saved, then he need not be circumcised because circumcision or not being circumcised means nothing to God. Obeying God's commands is what counts. (1 Corinthians 7:18–19)

If a slave becomes a Christian, then he should serve God in the place where he was saved. If a person can be free, then he should use his new position to serve God. Even the slave who becomes a Christian is free in his spirit, but he is a slave to Christ. (1 Corinthians 7:21–22)

If you were bought with a price of Christ's blood, then you belong to Christ. (1 Corinthians 7:23)

If you live to buy things, then you should live as though you possessed nothing. (1 Corinthians 7:30)

If you have to do business in the world, then you should not become attached to it because this world is passing away. (1 Corinthians 7:31)

If you are an unmarried woman, then you can devote yourself to God since you are concerned about being holy in body and spirit. But the married woman has to be concerned about pleasing God and her husband. (1 Corinthians 7:34)

If anyone feels they must marry, because they have trouble disciplining their desires, then they should marry and it is not sin. If a person has self-control, and decides not to marry, then they have made a wise choice. (1 Corinthians 7:36–37)

If you marry, then you are living in God's will, and the one who doesn't marry can then serve God better. (1 Corinthians 7:38)

If a woman's husband dies, then she is free to marry again but she must only marry in the Lord. (1 Corinthians 7:39)

If anyone says he has all the answers, then he is just showing how little he knows. But the one who loves God and does His will, then he is the one God knows. (1 Corinthians 8:2–3)

If you are a runner in a race, then you try to win. I will always try to win the race for Christ. (1 Corinthians 9:24)

If I think that I would never do these things, then I must take heed lest I fall into their trap. (1 Corinthians 10:12)

If I drink the communion cup that represents the blood of Christ, then I receive a blessing from You. And I also receive a blessing when I eat the bread that represents the body of Christ that was broken for me. (1 Corinthians 10:16–17)

If a non-Christian invites me to a meal, then I'll go eat what is served, but I won't ask any questions for conscience's sake. (1 Corinthians 10:27)

If I am a believer, then I won't use my freedom to hurt a weaker Christian, and I won't let his conscience limit me. I won't do only what pleases me, or what's best for me; I will do what is best so others will be saved. (1 Corinthians 10:30, 33)

If a man refuses to remove his hat when he prays or preaches the Scriptures, then he dishonors his head—Christ. (1 Corinthians 11:4)

If a believer eats this bread and drinks this cup, then every time he does it, he relives the truth of the gospel. The Lord's Table is a memorial until He comes. (1 Corinthians 11:26)

If I eat the bread and drink the cup in an unworthy manner, then I am guilty of sin against the Lord's body and blood. Therefore, I will examine myself thoroughly before eating the bread or drinking the cup because anyone who eats or drinks in an unworthily manner, not meditating on the body and blood of Christ, is contributing to his own condemnation. (1 Corinthians 11:27–28)

If a Christian is judged or punished, then it is so he won't be condemned with the unsaved. (1 Corinthians 11:32)

If there are people in the church who claim they are speaking messages from the Spirit of God, then how do you know if their messages are coming from God, or if they are just making up what they say? They can't claim to speak messages from You if they curse Jesus, and when they proclaim "Jesus is Lord," they are speaking Your message. (1 Corinthians 12:2–3)

If the Holy Spirit gives all these different spiritual gifts to different people just as He decides, then believers have the ability to use these gifts to get results in the lives of others. (1 Corinthians 12:11)

If all the parts of the body were the same, then how could the body function? There are many parts of the body, but it is still one body. The eye cannot say to the hand, if all the parts of the body were the same, then how could the body function? There are many parts of the body, but it is still one body. The eye cannot say to the hand, "I do not need you." Nor can the head say to the feet, "I do not need you." (1 Corinthians 12:19–20)

If one part suffers, then all parts suffer with it, and if one part is honored, then all parts enjoy it. (1 Corinthians 12:26)

If I am a member of Christ's body, then I am gifted differently from everyone else. The first place was given to apostles, second to prophets, third to teachers, and after them those who do miracles. Then comes the gift of healing, helping, and leadership, and last is speaking foreign languages. (1 Corinthians 12:27–28)

If I speak with the eloquence of great speakers, or if I speak in the languages of angels, but I didn't love others, then I'm simply making noise like cymbals clashing or a gong that rings. (1 Corinthians 13:1)

If I can predict the future, or understand Your mysteries, or if I know everything, or have faith to move mountains, but I don't love others, then I've accomplished nothing in life. (1 Corinthians 13:2)

If I gave everything I possess to the poor, and even sacrificed my body, but I didn't have love, then it would be of no value. (1 Corinthians 13:3)

If you prophesy, then you help others grow in Christ by motivating and instructing them. (1 Corinthians 14:3)

If Paul was using tongues in his prayers, then his spirit is praying to God though he didn't know what he was saying. If Paul would pray in tongues and he would pray in ordinary languages, then everyone understood and prayed with him. (1 Corinthians 14:14–15)

If a visitor heard everyone speaking a message he could understand, then he can be convicted by what he hears, and will have his secret thoughts exposed; then he will fall on his knees crying out to You, saying, "God indeed is among the church." (1 Corinthians 14:24–25)

If someone with the gift of interpretation is not present, then the tongues-speaker must keep quiet and speak only to God in private. (1 Corinthians 14:28)

If someone is preaching and another person receives something special from the Lord, then the preacher shall allow that one to speak, so the whole church will learn from God and be encouraged. (1 Corinthians 14:30–31)

If our Christian benefits are in this life only, then we have a miserable life. (1 Corinthians 15:19)

If I keep on diligently doing Your work, knowing my labor is not in vain, and You will keep me safe till the resurrection, then I will never give in and never admit defeat. (1 Corinthians 15:58)

Book of 2 Corinthians

If I am deeply hurting in every area of life, then Your promises greatly encourage me. (2 Corinthians 1:5)

If I forgive, then Satan doesn't have an advantage over me, for I am not ignorant of his strategy; he wants to discourage and defeat me. (2 Corinthians 2:11)

If we have our confidence in Christ, then none of us should brag about the results of our ministry because our ability comes from You. (2 Corinthians 3:4–5)

If I try to keep the law to be saved, then I will die because the Spirit gives me eternal life. (2 Corinthians 3:7)

If the gift of the law was glorious, then how much more glorious the giving of the grace of God? (2 Corinthians 3:9)

If the law that was temporary had some splendor, then how much more glorious is our heavenly hope in Your eternal plan of salvation? (2 Corinthians 3:10)

If Your Holy Spirit is working in hearts, and when the Spirit works in my life, then there is freedom to understand Your truth. (2 Corinthians 3:17)

If You give me a great ministry that I didn't deserve, then I will not falsely represent myself, nor will I hide the truth. I will declare Your truth to everyone so they can understand Your Word. (2 Corinthians 4:1–2)

If I have the treasure of Jesus Christ in my frail human body, then outsiders will see Your power and know it doesn't come from my weakness. (2 Corinthians 4:7)

If I have troubles everywhere I go, then I am not distressed, and I don't give up. I am persecuted, but not forsaken by You. I am knocked down, but not knocked out. If I even face death daily, then I serve Christ Jesus who went to death for sinners like me. (2 Corinthians 4:8–9)

If my life is renewed daily, then others can see the life of Christ shining through me.
(2 Corinthians 4:10)

If I speak what I believe, then may my life reflect what I speak. May I say what I believe. (2 Corinthians 4:13)

If I don't look at my present suffering, then I will look forward to being happy in heaven because things I see on earth last only for a short time, but the things I can't see with my physical eyes are eternal—they last forever. (2 Corinthians 4:18)

If my earthly body dies, then I have a spiritual body made by You alone. (2 Corinthians 5:1)

If I groan and get weary in this body, then it's better than not having a body at all. Yet when I get to heaven, then I'll have a new body, and I won't lose this present body, but it will be transformed into an eternal body. (2 Corinthians 5:4–5)

If I live in this present body, then I must live by faith, which is obeying Your principles, not living to please the body. (2 Corinthians 5:7)

If I think of His death, that Christ died for all sinners, then the love of Christ overwhelms me. (2 Corinthians 5:14)

If He died for all, then all died with Him, so that I should no longer live for myself but for Him who died and was raised to new life. (2 Corinthians 5:15)

If I have received Christ into my life, then You have created me as a new person in Christ, the old life is gone; now I have a new life in Him. (2 Corinthians 5:17)

If I do anything to discredit myself, then I might make it hard for people to get saved. I will do the opposite and do everything I can to bring people to Christ. (2 Corinthians 6:3–4)

If I want to be pure, patient, kind, loving, and knowledgeable of Your principles, then I can minister in the Holy Spirit's power, according to the Word of God, clothed in the armor of righteousness. (2 Corinthians 5:6–7)

If there is no agreement between Your temple and idols, then I won't let unbelievers control my life. (2 Corinthians 6:16)

If You want me to separate myself from unsaved people and not touch dirty things, then You can welcome me and be my Father, and all believers will be Your sons and daughters as You have promised. (2 Corinthians 6:18)

If I separate myself from evil, whether it touches my body or spirit, then I will be completely holy unto You, living in reverence to You. (2 Corinthians 7:1)

If Godly sorrow leads to repentance for salvation, then I will never regret this type of sorrow that drives me back to You. (2 Corinthians 7:10)

If anyone wants to boast, then let him boast in You, our Father. Then it's not a matter of self-approval, but of having Your approval. (2 Corinthians 10:17–18)

If anyone preached about another Jesus that was different from the one Paul preached, then they would quickly embrace any false teacher because they were gullible about their faith. Also they would quickly embrace a false spirit, different from the One they got at salvation. (2 Corinthians 11:5)

Book of Galatians

If anyone preaches a gospel contrary to what the Galatians believed, then let him be under a curse forever. (Galatians 1:9)

If Paul catered to people, then he'd not be Christ's servant; he wanted Your approval not to please people. (Galatians 1:10)

If I was crucified with Christ; then I died when He died on the cross, so I no longer try to live for God in the flesh. Now Christ lives within me to give me new life. (Galatians 2:20)

If those who try to keep the law, don't keep all the law, then they are under the curse that comes with the law, for if legalists don't keep all the law, then they will be judged by the curse promised in Scripture. No one ever got saved by obeying the law. (Galatians 3:10–11)

If You promised to save those who exercise faith, then You cannot change or cancel that promise. (Galatians 3:16)

If we once have faith in Christ Jesus, then we don't need the law's authority. (Galatians 3:25)

If we have faith in Christ Jesus, then we are the children of God. (Galatians 3:26)

If we were baptized into Christ, then we became a part of His family; we put on Christ and become like Him. (Galatians 3:27)

If I belong to Christ, then I am a true heir to the promises made to Him. (Galatians 3:29)

If I am Your child, then You have sent the Spirit of Christ into my heart so I can talk to You, saying, "Abba Father." I am no longer a slave, but Your very own. If I am Your child, then You have sent the Spirit of Christ into my heart so I can talk to You, saying, "Abba Father." I am no longer a slave, but Your very own child. And If I am Your child, then all spiritual blessings belong to me. (Galatians 4:6–7)

If I love them and pray compassionately for them, then they will be encouraged and grow in Christ. (Galatians 4:15)

If I was born again by the Spirit of God, then You give me a new nature to obey You, which is a much greater motive to do the right thing than trying to keep the law to please You. (Galatians 4:26)

If anyone tries to be justified by keeping the law, then he cuts himself off from the life of Christ, and has fallen from grace. (Galatians 5:4)

If I have been called to freedom in Christ, then I am not called to freedom to follow my sinful nature, but am free to serve others in love. (Galatians 5:13)

If I will live in the Spirit, then I will not satisfy the lust of my sinful nature. (Galatians 5:16)

If I am controlled by the Spirit, then I am no longer a legalist. (Galatians 5:18)

II you indulge in sexual immorality, impure thoughts, sensuality, worship of false gods, spiritism (Galatians contacting demons), hating people, attacking people, jealousy of others, anger at everything, drunkenness, wild parties, and things like these, then you will not see the kingdom of God. (Galatians 5:19–21)

If I live by the direction of the Spirit, then I can produce the fruit of the Spirit. (Galatians 5:25)

If I am not ambitious for my own reputation, then I won't be making others jealous, but Christ will be the passion of my life. (Galatians 5:26)

If I see a fellow Christian overtaken by sin, then I will humbly try to get him on the right path. I will not feel superior to him, but will guard myself against all temptations. (Galatians 6:1)

If people think they are important, but they are really nobody, then they end up deceiving themselves. (Galatians 6:3)

If everyone does their part to do their very best in all things, then they can have personal satisfaction. If we do something worthwhile, then we won't have to depend on the approval of others. (Galatians 6:4)

If someone sows to his sinful nature, then his harvest will be death and destruction; but if they sow to the Holy Spirit, then their harvest will be everlasting life. (Galatians 6:8)

If I will not get tired of doing good things, then I will reap a good harvest if I don't give up. (Galatians 6:9)

If believers live by the power of the Spirit, then Your peace and mercy is on all believers and all who belong to You. (Galatians 6:16)

Book of Ephesians

If you put your trust in His salvation, then you will receive the great spiritual inheritance that He planned according to His infinite purpose that He has for each one. (Ephesians 1:11)

If you put your trust in God when you heard the message of God's truth—the gospel—then that delivered you and you were sealed by the Holy Spirit who guaranteed your eternal life until you come into possession of it at the rapture or death; it will thus bring You glory. (Ephesians 1:13–14)

If I trust in You, then I have a love for all Your people and have continually given thanks to You in my prayers, asking that You would give me full wisdom and understanding so I can have full knowledge of You. (Ephesians 1:15–16)

If I want to understand the hope to which You call me, then I ask that You open the eyes of my heart to see the glorious riches of my inheritance that You have given to me. (Ephesians 1:17–18)

If I am rich in mercy, then it is because of Your great love for me. (Ephesians 2:4)

If I put my faith in You, then I am saved by grace for it was not my own doing, but Your gift to me. I cannot say that I had anything to do with it. (Ephesians 2:8–9)

If you are His followers, then you are being built with other believers into a building a sanctuary where the Father lives by the Holy Spirit. (Ephesians 2:22)

If I have to go through troubles and persecutions, then I am not discouraged; rather I am honored and encouraged that I can be a testimony to the truth. (Ephesians 3:11–12)

If I have faith in You, then I can come fearlessly into Your presence, knowing You will receive me and listen to my request. (Ephesians 3:13)

If I am accepted in Christ, then I am accepted, and I fall on my knees before You, the Father, the Creator of heaven and earth, praying that Your power will give me inner strength through the Holy Spirit so that Christ can make His home in my heart by faith and that I'll be rooted and grounded in His love. (Ephesians 3:14–17)

If I pray to fully experience Your love—even though it is beyond understanding—then I can be filled with all the fullness that comes only from You. (Ephesians 3:19)

If we live under Your direction, then each part of the body will help others grow so that all of us become mature believers, and the whole body becomes mature in love for one another. (Ephesians 4:16)

If I no longer live the way the ungodly live, then it's because they do not understand Your ways for their minds are spiritually blinded and they are far away from You, the Father, because they have shut their minds to the truth and resisted Your will. (Ephesians 4:17–19)

If I put away lying, then I will tell everyone the truth because we are related to one another in Your body. (Ephesians 4:22)

If I am spiritually renewed in my thoughts and attitudes the way You told me to, then I can put on the new nature which You created to be godly, righteous, and holy. (Ephesians 4:23–24)

If I don't stop being angry and sinning against others, and if I do not let the sun go down on my wrath, then my anger gives room for the enemy to get into my life. (Ephesians 4:25–27)

If the Holy Spirit has sealed me with the authority of His presence that will keep me until the final day of redemption, then I will not give grief to the Holy Spirit by living a sinful life. I will get rid of all bitterness, rage, name-calling, mean-spirited retaliation, slander; instead I will be kind to others, tenderhearted, forgiving others as You, Father, forgave me because of Christ. (Ephesians 4:30–32)

If sexual sins or dirty actions or greed are contrary to Godliness, then I will not be involved in them. Also I will not be known by filthy speech, foolish talking, and jesting, but I will be gracious in all things. (Ephesians 5:3–4)

If I drink wine, then I will lose control of myself, instead I will let the Holy Spirit continually fill me and control me. (Ephesians 5:18)

If I put on Your spiritual armor, then I can stand against the deceptive strategy of the enemy for I am not fighting against humans who have flesh and blood, but against evil powers, authorities, and demons of the unseen world, mighty powers of darkness and their tricks. (Ephesians 6:10–12)

If evil comes, then I will use every piece of Your armor so I'll be able to resist and win the battle. With Your help, I'll stand in battle with Your truth buckled around my waist. I'll cover my chest with the armor of righteousness, and I'll wear the shoes of peace that come from the good news of the Gospel. I'll carry the shield of faith to stop all the arrows and fiery darts of Satan. I'll wear the protective helmet of salvation and I'll protect myself with the sword of the Spirit, which is the Word of God. I will pray at all times, with every type of intercession and spiritual warfare. I will pray persistently and boldly for all Christians everywhere. (Ephesians 6:13–18)

If I pray for those who minister for You, then they will have boldness and the right words to proclaim the message of the good news of the gospel. (Ephesians 6:19)

Book of Philippians

If my passion is to live for You, O Christ, then if I die, it will be my gain. If I go on living in this body, then I will still continue serving You. (Philippians 1:21–22)

If I remain on this earth or die, then I pray that my family and friends will continue living for You and they remain firm in their faith in the gospel. (Philippians 1:26–27)

If I do all things without murmuring and complaining, then I will be a blameless child of God in the eyes of all who live in a crooked evil world. May I shine as a light to them all. (Philippians 2:14–15)

If I share with others the Words of life, then it will help me be faithful until Christ returns. (Philippians 2:16)

If You help me run my race victoriously, then my works will not become useless. (Philippians 2:16)

If I die a martyr's death like Paul, then I will rejoice in this opportunity. May other believers rejoice with me if I have the privilege of dying for You. (Philippians 2:17–18)

If good or bad happens in my life, then I want to rejoice in Your provision for me. (Philippians 3:1)

If I give up everything for the knowledge of Christ, then I will no longer treasure them because Christ has become my treasure. (Philippians 3:8)

If I know that I have not attained the goal, and do not consider my life perfect, then I focus my entire energy on this one thing: I daily forget past accomplishments and failures and look forward to what lies ahead. I keep all my energy to win the prize of Your upward calling to me as Christ Jesus. (Philippians 3:13–14)

If we are spiritual believers, then we should all be doing the same thing, but many are not pursuing Christ. Everyone must live at the level they've learned and obey the truth they know. (Philippians 3:16)

If I rejoice gladly in all Your goodness, then You will always keep me filled with Your joy. (Philippians 4:4)

If Christ may come at any moment, then let my gentleness and goodness be evident to all because Christ may come at any moment. I won't worry about anything, but I'll pray to You about everything, and I'll be thankful for all things that happen; then Your peace will guard my heart and mind because the presence of Christ Jesus in my life surpasses anything that I could ever understand. (Philippians 4:5–7)

Book of Colossians

If I pray for spiritual wisdom, then I will make decisions that will honor and please You. (Colossians 1:9)

If I pray to continually do good things for others, then I am obedient to Your command to me. (Colossians 1:10)

If I pray to know You more intimately, then I can enjoy fellowship with You. (Colossians 1:10)

If I pray to be strengthened with spiritual power, then I can endure with patience from You. (Colossians 1:11)

If I pray to be filled with joy, then I'll always be thankful for the spiritual inheritance You've given me. (Colossians 1:12)

If I am motivated to serve You, Christ, then it is because You energize the Father's work within me. (Colossians 1:29)

If I know that only Christ is the wisdom of God, then may no one deceive me with cunning arguments that anyone is the wisdom of God. (Colossians 2:4)

If I am rooted in the faith, and nourished by Christ, then I'll grow strong in my Christian life, and may I always be thankful for what Christ has done for me. (Colossians 2:7)

If a believer was indwelt by Christ, then the believer could experience Your full understanding and leadership. (Colossians 2:10)

If I am completely forgiven, then no one can condemn me for what I eat or drink, or for not celebrating holy days or Sabbaths. (Colossians 2:16)

If I have been raised to new life in Christ, then I will control my thinking by the principles of heaven where Christ is sitting at Your right hand in the seat of honor and influence. (Colossians 3:1)

If I now have Christ dwelling in my life, then I will get rid of anger, rebellious behavior, slander, and filthy language. (Colossians 3:8)

If You chose me to live a holy life, then I will clothe myself with mercy, kindness, humility, gentleness, and patience. I recognize that some believers let these sins disrupt their lives, so I will forgive their trespasses as You forgave me. (Colossians 3:12–13)

If I put on love because it is the most important attitude, then love makes me one with all believers. (Colossians 3:14)

If I want the rich words of Christ to live in my heart, then I have His wisdom to teach and correct other believers. (Colossians 3:16)

If wives submit to their husbands, then it is because that is what You desire of them. (Colossians 3:18)

If husbands must love their wives, then they will never be mean to them. (Colossians 3:19)

If children must obey their parents, then it is because it pleases You. (Colossians 3:20)

If servants must obey their earthly bosses, then that means in everything, not just when they are watching. They must obey from the heart, because that pleases You. (Colossians 3:22)

If I do everything with my whole heart, then it is because I am working to please You, and not men. (Colossians 3:23)

If you do wrong, then you will be repaid for your rebellion because God will not let anyone get away with sin. (Colossians 3:25)

If you are a master who directs servants, then you must be kind and fair, just as God, our Master in heaven, treats us. (Colossians 4:1)

Book of 1 Thessalonians

If you are a believer, then ask the Lord to help you be gentle among new believers as Paul was unassuming and kind to the Thessalonians. The Lord will help you care for young followers of Christ to feed and protect them as a mother cares for her baby, and to love new Christians, willing to give them your own soul as well. (1 Thessalonians 2:7–8)

If Your work prospers in spite of trials, then I cannot thank You enough for all the joy I have in Your presence. (1 Thessalonians 3:9)

If I have trials, then I pray that You, the Father of our Lord Jesus Christ, will help me stand in the face of them. (1 Thessalonians 3:11)

If there are those suffering persecution, then may You make my love grow and overflow to those who are suffering. (1 Thessalonians 3:12)

If the saints who are Yours are returning with Jesus Christ, then make my heart strong, blameless, and holy before You, the Father of us all, and may I live a guiltless life. (1 Thessalonians 3:13)

If You want me to be separate from sin and to especially keep away from sexual immorality, then teach me that I should please You with my daily life and command me to live as close as possible to the Biblical standards in the Scriptures. (1 Thessalonians 4:1–3)

If I marry, then You want me to marry in holiness and purity and not in sexual lust as do the pagans for this is a sign they do not know God. (1 Thessalonians 4:4–5)

If you have sex with another's spouse, then God has promised to punish this sin. (1 Thessalonians 4:6)

If anyone rebels against the rule of purity, then he is not disobeying man's laws, he is disobeying Your law and rebelling against the Holy Spirit who dwells in him. (1 Thessalonians 4:8)

If you want to influence those who are not Christians, then your goal is to live a quiet life, to work diligently at your task, and do faithfully all you are required to do and have enough money to live on. (1 Thessalonians 4:11–12)

If we believe that Jesus died for us and rose from the dead, then those who have died and sleep in Jesus will be brought with Him at His return. If we are alive at His return, then we will not be raptured before those in graves, but they will be raptured first. (1 Thessalonians 4:14–15)

If you are alive and remain on the earth when Christ returns, then you will be caught up with those who are dead in the clouds to meet the Lord Jesus in the air, to ever live with Him because His promise assures you that you'll live with Him forever. (1 Thessalonians 4:16–18)

If this is what You expect me to do, then I'll give thanks always to You for everything. I'll not suppress the Holy Spirit's work in my life and will listen to the preaching of Your Word. I won't be gullible; I will analyze everything by the Word of God to determine what is true. I'll stay away from every form of evil and anything that tempts me to sin. (1 Thessalonians 5:22)

Book of 2 Thessalonians

If I have constant determination, then it will demonstrate that Your care of me is correct and that I am worthy of the kingdom of God, for which I am now suffering. (2 Thessalonians 1:5)

If you persecute believers, then You will repay them and reward those who are suffering with the same inner confidence and peace we'll all receive when Jesus appears from heaven with His powerful angels. (2 Thessalonians 1:6–7)

If they reject the Lord and refuse to accept the good news of the Lord Jesus, then He will come in flaming fire to punish them. They will be punished in everlasting hell, forever separated from Your presence, never to see the glory of Your kingdom. (2 Thessalonians 1:8–9)

If you are one of the lost people, then the Antichrist will be Satan's representative—full of demonic power and lying tricks, one who will deceive all the lost people who don't have spiritual insight because they have already rejected the truth, and have chosen not to believe it. (2 Thessalonians 2:9–10)

If you refuse to believe His truth and choose willingly to sin, then you will be punished. (2 Thessalonians 2:12)

If any refuse to obey the command of Paul to never tire of doing the right thing, then I'll have nothing to do with them so they'll be convicted of their wrong ways. He is not an enemy to Christ, but a brother who needs correction. (2 Thessalonians 3:13–15)

Book of 1 Timothy

If you have drifted from a sincere heart, a pure conscience, and believing faith, then you are not walking in love and spend your time arguing about nothing. (1 Timothy 1:5–6)

If I apply the law properly to our lives, then I know the law is good for it is not given to keep good people in line, but the law is aimed at rebellious people to teach them the truth, and point them to salvation. The law is aimed at adulterers, perverts, slave traders, liars, and perjurers; it was written for those who deny the gospel and sound doctrine and the truth that was committed to Paul. (1 Timothy 1:8–11)

If you denied your conscience, then you have wrecked your faith because faith and a pure conscience are your weapons. (1 Timothy 1:19)

If you want to live peaceably and follow holiness and honesty in your life, then pray for political leaders and government supervisors. (1 Timothy 1:2)

If you fulfill your prayer obligation, then you will please your God and Savior because He wants everyone to be saved and to learn the full scope of Biblical truth. (1 Timothy 1:3–4)

If you are a woman, then Paul wanted women to dress modestly, without being indecent or calling undue attention to themselves. He wanted women to be noticed for their inner Godly personality, not for outward dress or fixing their hair, or gaudy jewels, or indiscreet clothing. He wanted women to do good works and listen to good Christian women so they could be Godly. (1 Timothy 2:9–10)

If any man wants to be a pastor/leader to do noble work for You, then he must be a good man: blameless, the husband of one wife, self-disciplined, hardworking, obedient, courteous, a good teacher, one who opens his home to visitors and guests. He can't drink alcohol or be hot-tempered, or greedy for money. He must be courteous and gentle, manage his family well, and not be a new convert. (1 Timothy 3:1–6)

If you are a deacon, then you should live by the same standard as the pastor of your church. (1 Timothy 3:7)

If you are wives of pastors and deacons, then you must be respectable and not be gossipers, but rather be faithful in every area of life. (1 Timothy 3:11)

If you are a deacon, then you should be the husband of one wife, lead happy and obedient families, do a good job as deacons; you should then be respected by all in the church and God will reward you with His blessings for your faithful walk in Christ Jesus. (1 Timothy 3:12–13)

If there are false teachers, then they will lie about the truth, and are hypocrites whose consciences are seared as though they were branded with a red-hot iron. They will forbid marriage and demand that people abstain from food. You've created every good food to eat, and I should reject no food, but I must thankfully enjoy it all, bless it and give thanks, and Your Scripture and prayer make it holy. (1 Timothy 4:2–5)

If you do spiritual exercise unlimited, then it rewards you with a good life here on earth and will reward you in heaven. (1 Timothy 4:9)

If I believe Christ died for me and lives forever, then I will give myself diligently to ministry and will take whatever suffering comes so that people will believe in Christ because my hope is in Him. (1 Timothy 4:10)

If I fulfill Your calling for my life, then I will be careful of what I do and teach so that people who hear me will be saved. (1 Timothy 4:16)

If you are a relative of a widow, then you must take care of her and not expect the church to do it. Then the church can use its money to care for needy widows who fit the qualifications of genuine widows. (I Timothy 5:16)

If pastors preach and teach well, then the church is to give worthy pastors double consideration in paying them. (1 Timothy 5:17)

If there are two or three witnesses, then you can listen to complaints against the church leaders and if the church leaders are wrong, rebuke them in front of the church as a warning to all believers. (1 Timothy 5:19–20)

If you are a worker, then you must not take advantage of your boss because he is a Christian, but Christian workers must do better since they are helping their bosses make their businesses effective and successful. (1 Timothy 6:1–2)

If I am happy and satisfied with what You give, then I am truly rich. (1 Timothy 6:6)

If you are passionate about being rich, then you are open to all types of temptations and get-rich-quickly schemes. Your financial lust will hurt your walk with Christ and eventually destroy your life. (1 Timothy 6:9)

If I am dedicated to You Lord, then I will avoid the evils associated with money. I purpose to live a saintly life and I will seek to be filled with faith, love, and gentleness, and I will fight to put You first in all my life. (1 Timothy 6:11–12)

If I promised to do all that I say I will do, then no one can find any fault in me both now and in the future till Christ returns. (1 Timothy 6:14)

If you are rich in this world, then you should not look down on others, or trust in your money, but trust in God, who out of His riches gives us all we need to be happy. (1 Timothy 6:17)

If you are rich, then use your money to do good; be rich in good works, generous and willing to share with those in need. (1 Timothy 6:18)

If you want the only safe investment in life, then store up real wealth in heaven. (1 Timothy 6:19)

Book of 2 Timothy

If I have the help of the Holy Spirit, then I will guard Your special calling for my life because the Holy Spirit lives in me. (2 Timothy 1:14)

If I communicate to trustworthy people all the truth I heard from my teachers, then they in turn will be able to reach others. (2 Timothy 2:2)

If an athlete cannot win a contest unless he keeps all the rules, then I will discipline myself to obey Christ. (2 Timothy 2:5)

If a farmer gets first claim on the harvest over any crops growing in his field, then I will work hard to get Your reward. (2 Timothy 2:6–7)

If I hold firm in my profession of faith, then I will reign with Him in glory. If I deny Christ, then He will deny me. (2 Timothy 2:12–13)

If I study to know everything about Christianity, then I can be Your approved workman. (2 Timothy 2:15)

If I seek holiness, faith, love, and peace in fellowship with all who call on the Lord, then I will not give into the lust of youth. (2 Timothy 2:22)

If I choose not to quarrel with anyone, then I will instead be kind, a good teacher, and patient with all. (2 Timothy 2:24)

If I correct people who disagree with me, then I will be gentle when I correct them, remembering You can change their minds so that they will recognize the truth, and escape Satan's grip on them, and be free of his trap. (2 Timothy 2:25–26)

If in the last days before Christ comes, there may be dangerous times as people will be aggressively self-centered and greedy for money; they will also be boastful, arrogant, and will scoff at You. They will be contentious and ungrateful to their parents, lack any sensitivity for people, be inhumane, act without love and forgiveness, be sarcastic, violent, rebellious, hate anything good, be treacherous, rash, conceited, and addicted to pleasure, rather than serving as lovers of God. If so, then I won't have anything to do with these people, and I'll keep away from them. (2 Timothy 3:1–5)

If I read the Bible, which was written by Your inspiration, teaches me the truth, and points out what is wrong in my life, then it is helping me do what is right. The Bible is Your tool to prepare me in every area of my life, so I can do Your work. I will preach Your Word continually, at every place, at all times, when it is suitable and when it is not. I will correct false teaching and rebuke those who do not believe and I will encourage all people to do the right thing all the time, based on what Your Word teaches. (2 Timothy 3:16–17; 4:2)

If people won't listen to the truth, then they will seek out teachers who reinforce their sin and they won't listen to Your Word, but will live by their misguided, rebellious ways. (2 Timothy 4:3–4)

If I have fought the good fight to the end, run the race to the finish line, and kept true to the faith, then I expect the crown of righteousness that You reserve for faithful witnesses will be given to all who look for Christ's appearing. (2 Timothy 4:7–8)

Book of Titus

If you are a pastor, then you must have unquestioned character and be the husband of one wife, your children must be believers, and you must not be charged with disorderly conduct. You must be blameless, never arrogant, short-tempered, violent, greedy, or a brawler; instead, you must be hospitable, friendly, self-disciplined, fair-minded, and dedicated. (Titus 1:6–8)

If you are committed to purity, then you will find purity in your search for truth. Those who are rebellious and evil in their thinking will find the corruption they seek. (Titus 1:15)

If you are an older woman, then you must be holy in behavior, must not gossip or get drunk, be a teacher of Godliness, teaching younger women to behave rightly, love their husbands, and love their children. (Titus 2:3–4)

If you are a younger woman, then you must be sexually pure, gentle, keep your house clean, obey your husband so you don't disgrace the Gospel with your lifestyle. (Titus 2:5)

If you are a younger man, then you should behave, be serious about your duties in life, be an example of sincerity and honesty, and keep your promises so no one can accuse you of lying; you must not take advantage of others financially. (Titus 2:6–8)

If you are a worker, then you should be obedient to your bosses, obey the orders given you, and never steal anything from them, but be completely honest at all times. (Titus 2:9)

If I am a Christian, then I will be obedient to government officials, and will obey all civic laws, and I'll work honestly for a living. I will not slander government rulers, nor will I pick fights with them. I will be courteous to them and be kind to all people. (Titus 3:1–2)

If you are saved, then it is because the Lord revealed His kindness and love to save you; you were not saved by your works of righteousness, but you were saved by His mercy. He washed away your sins and you were born again by the working of the Holy Spirit in your life, which He abundantly poured out to you through Jesus Christ your Savior. (Titus 3:4–6)

If I rely on Your truth and affirm it constantly, then they who believe in You for salvation will be careful to maintain good works. This truth is good and it works for me, and will work for all who believe it. (Titus 3:8)

If you are a believer, then you should help others who have need, as this makes their lives productive. (Titus 3:14)

Book of Hebrews

If I pay careful attention to the Biblical things I've heard, then I won't drift away from You. (Hebrews 2:1)

If the message spoken by angels was true, and every disobedience has its own judgment, then no one will go unpunished if he neglects Your salvation that is promised to him. (Hebrews 2:2)

If I hear Your voice speaking to me, then I will not stubbornly resist You as Israel rebelled against You and wandered in the desert for 40 years. (Hebrews 3:7–8)

If my heart is hardened and I refuse to obey You, then I shall never enter into the rest You have for me. (Hebrews 3:11)

If I listen to Your Word today, then I won't develop an unbelieving stubborn heart. (Hebrews 3:13)

If I faithfully trust You to the end, just as when I was first saved, then I can share in all the blessings You have planned for me. (Hebrews 3:14)

If Your promise of entering Your rest still stands, then I will be careful not to neglect entering Your rest. (Hebrews 4:1)

If you hear God's voice today, then He warns you to harden not your hearts against Him. (Hebrews 4:7)

If Your Word is alive and active, sharper than a two-edged sword, piercing the unseen things such as my soul and spirit, then it is exposing my thoughts and attitudes for what they are. (Hebrews 4:12)

If I come boldly to Your throne, then I will receive mercy and find grace in my hour of need. (Hebrews 4:16)

If I show the same diligence to the very end of life, then I will get my full reward when I get to heaven. I will not become lazy, but will follow the example of those who through faith and patience received the prize. (Hebrews 6:11–12)

If I believe Your promise and Your oath since it's impossible for You to lie, then I know without a doubt that I'll receive the eternal life You've promised. (Hebrews 6:18)

If my heart is clean by the blood of Christ, then I will draw near to You with a true heart and confident faith. (Hebrews 10:21)

If those who rejected the law of Moses were killed without mercy, then how much more severely will those be punished who trample underfoot the Son of God, and considered His blood of the new covenant as unworthy, and insulted the Spirit of God who worked in their hearts? (Hebrews 10:28–29)

If I persevere in doing Your will, then I will receive what You have promised. (Hebrews 10:36)

If I know that in a little while You will come and not be delayed, then I will do what the Scriptures say: "The just will live by faith and if he shrinks back, then I will have no pleasure in him." (Hebrews 10:37–38)

If I never turned back from following You, then my faith assures me that my soul will be saved. (Hebrews 10:39)

If because of my faith I am sure You will answer my request, then my faith makes me certain about the things I can't see. (Hebrews 11:1)

If I have not forgotten Your words of encouragement to me, then I will not be discouraged when the Lord rebukes me or lightly chastens me because the Lord disciplines those He loves, and punishes everyone He acknowledges as His child. (Hebrews 12:5–6)

If anyone is not corrected by You, then he is not Your child. He is an illegitimate child, and not Your true child. (Hebrews 12:8)

If I am punished it isn't enjoyable at the time I receive it, then it makes me live right and submit to the laws of men so that I will live in peace and develop character. (Hebrews 12:11)

If I hold up under Your discipline, then I won't be weak, but strong. I'll stand firm on shaky legs and those who follow me will not stumble, but will walk strong. (Hebrews 12:12–13)

If I don't do everything possible to live peaceably with everyone, and live a holy life, then without that, no one will see You. (Hebrews 12:14)

If I am a part of the kingdom that is unshakeable, then I will serve You with thankfulness. (Hebrews 12:28)

If I am a Christian, then I will be concerned for those in prison, as though I was there, and I will remember those who are ill-treated because I know how they feel. I will honor the sanctity of the marriage vows because the marriage bed should be kept pure, and You will punish the adulterer and sexually immoral people. I will live free from greedy lust for money and be content with what I have. (Hebrews 13:3–5)

If my church leaders give an account to You of how well they watch over my soul and others, then I will continue to obey them and follow their directions. I will obey them so they will enjoy their ministry because I would be the loser if I caused them grief. (Hebrews 13:17)

Book of James

If I lack wisdom, then I will ask You for it because You liberally give us spiritual understanding and I know I will receive it from You. But I must ask with unwavering faith because those who are unstable are like the unpredictable waves of the ocean, driven by the wind. (James 1:5–6)

If a man is vacillating, then he will not receive anything from You because a double-minded person is unstable in everything. (James 1:7–8)

If I humble myself and take a low position, then You will lift me up for Your purpose. (James 1:9)

If you exalt yourselves as the rich, then you will be like the flower that is temporally here, then dies and is gone. Because the sun can burn flowers and they wither with the grass, their beauty is destroyed in the same scorching heat. (James 1:10–11)

If I endure the trials that try me, then You will bless me and I will receive the crown of life for enduring persecution which You have promised to those who continually love You. (James 1:12)

If I am tempted to give up, then I can't say You tempt me for You do not tempt anyone to evil actions. People are tempted by their own sinful desires that drag them away and entice them to sin. (James 1:13–14)

If evil lust is planted and grown, then it brings forth sin; and when sin is fully grown, it brings death. (James 1:15)

If I merely listen to the Word, then that is not enough; I will do what it says. (James 1:22)

If you merely listen to the Word and don't obey it, then you are like people who look at themselves in a mirror and forget what they see. (James 1:23–24)

If I want to look intently into the perfect law of liberty, then I know You will bless me if I don't forget what I see there and continue to obey what I learn there. (James 1:25)

If you appear to be religious and can't control your speech, then your religion is empty. (James 1:26)

If I want to have pure religion and be clean before You, then I must minister to the needs of orphans and widows and keep myself unspotted from the world. (James 1:27)

If I accept everyone equally before You, then I will not segregate myself for any person. I will not show partiality to those who are rich or finely dressed, nor will I look down on those who are poor and dirty. (James 2:1–2)

If I accept only people in rich apparel and reject the poor by making them sit in a segregated place or stand in the back of the crowd, then You will not bless me. (James 2:2–3)

If you show partiality, then you are judged by their evil thoughts, but I will accept people equally, and I reject those who segregate themselves against any. (James 2:4)

If you despise the poor, then you will eventually have some rich man oppress them and deliver them to judgment. These rich men blaspheme the very name of Christ, if you despise the poor, then you will eventually have some rich man oppress them and deliver them to judgment. These rich men blaspheme the very name of Christ, by whom all believers are called. (James 2:6–7)

If I reject anyone, then I am guilty of sin and I have broken the law. (James 2:9)

If I keep the whole law but break just one point, then I have broken all the law. You said, "Do not commit adultery," and "Do not kill," but if I do not commit adultery, but I kill, then I am a transgressor of the whole law. (James 2:10–11)

If I don't have good works to go with my faith, then I know it is not good to minister by faith. (James 2:14)

If a brother or sister doesn't have bread and is naked, and I say, "Go in peace, be fed and clothed," but I don't give them what they need, then what good is my faith? (James 2:15)

If my faith doesn't result in good works, then it is dead because it has no fruit. (James 2:17)

If I tell anyone, "You have faith and I have works," then he will try to show me his faith without works, and I will show him my faith by my works. (James 2:18)

If a body without a soul is dead, then faith without works is also dead or useless. (James 2:26)

If anyone doesn't offend by his speech, then he is perfect because he controls his mouth and he controls his whole body. (James 3:2)

If a little flame can start a forest fire, then so can my tongue spread sin throughout my body. So my tongue can defile my entire life, not realizing it is a fire from hell. (James 3:6)

If out of your mouth come blessings and curses, then this is wrong. (James 3:10)

If there is a wise man, then I want to see his wisdom in his conversation with other people; I want to see his meekness and wisdom by the things he says. (James 3:13)

If you are bitter and envious and start arguments, then you are full of self-glory and you lie against the truth. Their wisdom doesn't come from heaven; it comes from the earth, and it is fleshly and devilish because they produce arguments and confusion and evil. (James 3:14–16)

If you give me the wisdom that is from above; then it is pure, peaceable, gentle, and it will listen to others. I want wisdom that is full of mercy and good fruits, impartial to anyone and not hypocritical. I want the fruit of righteousness that is sown in peace; I want to be a peacemaker. (James 3:17–18)

If I fight with other believers, then it's because these battles come from our old nature that makes Christians fight one another. (James 4:1)

If I lust, then I don't get what I want. People destroy others and don't get what they want; they fight and argue and still don't get what things they want. (James 4:2)

If I don't ask rightly, then I do not have what I pray for because I ask wrongly to satisfy my lust. (James 4:3)

If you commit adultery, then you are friends of the world and they hate You. Help me realize those who are friends of the world are Your enemies. (James 4:4)

If I know the Holy Spirit in me has a strong desire that I live a holy and Godly life, then let the Spirit give me more grace to repent of evil. (James 4:5)

If I humble myself, then You give me grace, but You resist those who are proud. (James 4:6)

If I will submit myself to You, I will resist the devil so that he will flee from me, and then I'll have power from You. (James 4:7)

If I draw near to You, then You will draw near to me. I will cleanse my hands from sin, and I will purify my heart from double-minded thinking. I will be sad and mourn over my sin, and I won't laugh over it either because sin is a serious thing. I will humble myself in Your sight, then You can lift me up. (James 4:8–10)

If you say evil things about a believer and judge a believer, then you actually hate the law. (James 4:11)

If you will, then I will live, and I'll do certain things within Your plan for my life. (James 4:15)

If I know what good You want me to do, it's evil if I don't do it. (James 4:17)

If you are proud, then you will soon suffer misery; and you ought to weep and moan for coming judgment. (James 5:1)

If the rich live in pleasure and fulfill their lust, and they condemn and 'eat up' just people who do not resist them, then the rich have only fattened themselves for slaughter. (James 5:5–6)

If you are poor, then you must be patient until He comes, just as the farmer waits through the spring and fall rain for his crops to grow. The poor must wait for Your coming judgment. (James 5:7–8)

If you are enduring suffering patiently, then the Lord is very tender and kind to you. (James 5:11)

If I am not patient, then help me endure all my circumstances. I will not swear in trials or pain neither by heaven or earth; I will let my "Yes" mean "Yes" and my "No" mean "No" because I don't want to be condemned by my speech. (James 5:12)

If I am afflicted, then I will pray. If I am wrongly merry, then I'll read the Psalms to understand the severity of life. (James 5:13)

If I am sick, then I will call for the elders of the church so they can pray over me and anoint me with oil in Your name. I know the prayer of faith will save the sick and You will raise them up. (James 5:14–15)

If the sick will confess their sins and pray one for another, then the sick will be healed and when they have committed sins, then they will be forgiven. (James 5:16)

If you are a righteous man, then your continuous, sincere prayers will accomplish much. (James 5:16)

If any believer strays from the truth and is restored by another believer, then they not only turn around a sinner from his error, but they save a soul from death and hide a multitude of sins. (James 5:19–20)

Book of 1 Peter

If I have to suffer all kinds of trials on earth, then I am truly glad this wonderful hope is ahead and I know that when Jesus Christ is revealed, my faith, though tested, will be genuine like gold, and will bring praise and glory to You when Jesus Christ returns to earth. (1 Peter 1:6–7)

If I love Christ even though I have never seen Him with my eyes, then not seeing Him, I trust Him more because He has filled me with joy that can only come from Him. I know my future reward for trusting Christ will be the salvation of my soul in the final day. (1 Peter 1:8–9)

If I will obey Your truth, then I will not be conformed to the evil desires that controlled my life before I was saved. I will live a holy life, just as You who called me to salvation are holy, because the Bible says: "Be holy because God is holy." (1 Peter 1:14–16)

If I know that You, my heavenly Father, has no favorites, then I will pray boldly with reverence, knowing You will judge all people fairly. (1 Peter 1:17)

If I know that this physical life will pass away as the grass that withers, and flowers that die, then I know Your Word stands forever, so I put my trust in this Word that was preached to me. (1 Peter 1:23–24)

If I want to taste Your goodness, then it is because I can grow to the fullness of salvation. (1 Peter 2:3)

If I put my whole trust in Him, then He becomes precious to me. (1 Peter 2:7)

If Christ is the primary cornerstone, then He is a stumbling block to the unsaved. (1 Peter 2:8)

If I behave honorably among unsaved people, then they can see for themselves my good works. (1 Peter 2:12)

If I submit myself to human institutions, then it is for Your sake, especially to government leaders because they are Your representatives to punish lawbreakers. (1 Peter 2:13–14)

If you are a Christian employee, then you must be respectful and obedient to your bosses, not only when the bosses are kind to you, but also when the bosses are cruel and demanding. (1 Peter 2:18)

If you put up with undeserved punishment for Christ's sake, then there is a reward for you. But there is no reward when you're punished because you've done something wrong and deserve punishment. (1 Peter 2:19)

If you accept punishment patiently and do your duty, even when you don't deserve punishment, then you will get your reward. (1 Peter 2:20)

If you are a married woman, you are to be obedient to your husband so that if he refuses to obey the Word of God, he may be won to Christ by his wife's Godly behavior because your holy life speaks louder than your words. (1 Peter 3:1–2)

If you are a husband, then you are to treat your wife with respect and honor her as the weaker vessel, because husband and wife are heirs together of the grace of life. If the husband does this, then his prayers will not be hindered. (1 Peter 3:7)

If you never repay wrong with wrong, or a curse with a curse, but repay a curse with a blessing because that is what You call me to do, then I will be blessed by Him. (1 Peter 3:9)

If you want a happy life and prosperity, then you will not let your tongue lie, and become deceitful. (1 Peter 3:10)

If anyone tries to hurt me even when I do good, then You will reward me and you will not be afraid of them or their threats. (1 Peter 3:14)

If I hold the Lord Jesus reverently in my heart, then if someone asks why I believe as I do, I'll tell him why I have my hope in Christ. (1 Peter 3:15)

If I give my answer with courtesy and respect, then when attackers curse me, they'll become ashamed when they see my exemplary life and conduct. I Peter 3:16

II it is Your will that I suffer, then it is better that I suffer for doing right than for doing wrong. (1 Peter 3:17)

If your unsaved friends think you are strange for not indulging yourself in the same evil activities they do, then they will laugh at you in scorn, but they will have to give account to God who judges the living and the dead, and then will be punished for the way they lived. (1 Peter 4:4–5)

If I love everyone, then love makes up for my faults, and I will feed and give hospitality to those who need it. (1 Peter 4:8–9)

If You call me to preach, then I will allow You to speak through me and if You lead me to help others, then I will do it in Your strength. (1 Peter 4:11)

If I will be glad that I can suffer as Christ did, then I will rejoice when His glory is revealed. (1 Peter 4:13)

If people curse and blaspheme me as a Christian, then I will have Your blessing resting on me. (1 Peter 4:14)

If I suffer as a Christian, then I will not be ashamed but will praise You that I bear Christ's name. (1 Peter 4:16)

If I will be judged for my failures, then how much more will the unsaved be judged? If the righteous will barely make it through judgment, then how much more punishment will the ungodly have? (1 Peter 4:17–18)

If I suffer for doing Your will, then I will keep doing right. I will trust my soul to You, the faithful Creator, for You will never fail me. (1 Peter 4:19)

If I bow before You, then You will lift me up. (1 Peter 5:6)

If I will be watchful for attacks from my enemy, Satan, who prowls as a hungry lion, looking for prey to feed on, then I will stand firm against Satan, knowing Christians throughout the world are undergoing all kinds of suffering. (1 Peter 5:8–9)

If I suffer for a while on this earth, then You who have grace will call me to eternal glory with Christ. (1 Peter 5:10)

If I stand firm, then it is because I am encouraged to learn how You bless believers who are going through the same kind of sufferings that try me. (1 Peter 5:12)

Book of 2 Peter

If I do the right thing in the right way, then I will add character to my faith; and if I add Bible knowledge to my character, then I will always know what to do to please You. (2 Peter 1:5)

If I add self-control to my biblical knowledge, then I will be steadfast in knowing and doing right; and if I will add Godliness to my steadfastness, then I'll have a basis for becoming more Godly. (2 Peter 1:6)

If I add brotherly love to my Godliness, then my Godly life results in a loving relationship to all. (2 Peter 1:7)

If I abound in these traits, then I will not be ineffective or unfruitful in my walk on this earth. (2 Peter 1:8)

If you are a Christian and don't have these Godly traits, then you are blind and have forgotten that your former sins have been forgiven. (2 Peter 1:9)

If I have been called to salvation, chosen by You, then I will be diligent to demonstrate Your call in my life. If I do all these things, then there is no danger that I will ever fall away into sin, and I will eventually be given admission to Your eternal kingdom to live forever with my Lord and Savior, Jesus Christ. (2 Peter 1:10–11)

If I understand and believe that no prophecy of Scripture can be interpreted and understood in isolation, then every verse must be interpreted in light of all Scripture because no word of prophecy was written by human initiative and all the words men wrote in the Bible were inspired by the Holy Spirit. (2 Peter 1:20–21)

If there are false prophets, then they will subtly introduce dangerous heresies, they will deny You who redeemed them, and eventually they will cause their own destruction. Many will follow their filthy immorality, and by their lives will discredit the truth of God. In their lust they will try to make many people their disciples, but their foolish arguments make their judgment inevitable. (2 Peter 2:1–3)

If people indulge in their lusts and despise authority, then I know Your judgment is reserved for them. These wicked are arrogant and presumptuous and they dare to scoff at the Glorious One, the Lord Jesus Christ. (2 Peter 2:10)

If these evil men who are as dumb as animals, which You gave us to eat and do our work, and they laugh at the great powers of the unseen world, then they will be destroyed in their own corruption and be destroyed with Satan and the demons of hell. (2 Peter 2:12)

If there are false teachers, then they are like wells without water, like storm clouds without rain. The dark underworld is reserved for them because their proud works tempt new converts to return to sin who have just escaped the pagan world, and they use lust to coax new believers back into sin; they may promise freedom, but they are slaves themselves because they are dominated by sin. (2 Peter 2:17–19)

If anyone escapes the pollution of this world and allows himself to be enslaved again, then his second state is worse than his first one. It would have been better if he never learned the way of holiness. He is like the dog that returns to his own vomit and the pig that is washed and returns to wallow in the mire. (2 Peter 2:20–22)

If some people think You are slow about keeping Your promises, as some measure slowness, but then I know You will keep Your promises in Your time because You do not want anyone to perish, but You want all people to repent and trust You for salvation. (2 Peter 2:9)

Book of 1 John

If I declare this message to everyone, then it is because I worship You because You are light and there is absolutely no darkness in You. (1 John 1:5)

If I tell people that I have fellowship with You and yet I walk in darkness, then I lie and deny the truth. If I walk in the light as You are the light, then I have fellowship with other believers, and the blood of Jesus Christ cleanses me of all my sins. (1 John 1:6–7)

If I tell people I have no sin in me, then I deceive myself, and I don't have Your truth. (1 John 1:8)

If I confess my sins, then You are faithful to forgive my sins, and cleanse me from all unrighteousness. (1 John 1:8)

If I were to say I've never sinned, then I make You a liar and Your Word doesn't control me. (1 John 1:10)

If I slip and sin once, then I know Jesus Christ stands at Your right hand to plead forgiveness for me. (1 John 2:1)

If I have confidence that I'm Your child, then it's because I keep Your commands. (1 John 2:3)

If those who say they know You don't keep Your commands, then they are liars and they don't have the truth. (1 John 2:4)

If I keep Your Word, then I have Your love in my heart, and that's why I know I am Your child. (1 John 2: 5)

If I abide in You, then I ought to live the way You walked. (1 John 2:6)

If there are those who claim to be in the light but hate their brother, then they are in darkness until now. (1 John 1:9)

If there are those who love their brother and live in the light, then those persons will not stumble in darkness. (1 John 1:10)

If those who hate their brothers live in the darkness of sin, and walk in darkness, then they don't know what they're doing, because the darkness of sin has blinded their eyes. (1 John 1:11)

If you love the world, then you don't love God, the Father. (1 John 1:15)

If worldly attraction involves the lust of the flesh, the lust of the eyes, and the pride of life, then these are not from You, but are from the evil one. (1 John 1:16)

If I know the world will pass away, as well as fleshly lust, then I will live forever by doing Your will. (1 John 1:17)

If there are those who deny that Jesus is the Messiah, then they are liars, and they have the spirit of Antichrist because they deny both You the Father and the Son, and they don't have Your presence in their lives, but those who have the Son, also have You. (1 John 2:22–23)

If I continue in the message I heard from the beginning, and I continue abiding, then I will fellowship with You and the Son, and have the promise of eternal life. (1 John 2:24–25)

If I still have the anointing You gave me at salvation, then I don't need anyone to explain truth to me, because that anointing gives me basic spiritual understanding so I will abide in the truth that has been taught me. (1 John 2:27–28)

If all those who obey Him are born of God, then I know that Jesus Christ is righteous to them. (1 John 2:29)

If anyone who keeps on sinning breaks Your commands, then it is because sin is breaking Your law. (1 John 3:4)

If I stay close to Jesus, then I won't sin, and those who sin continually were not saved in the first place and they don't know Him. (1 John 3:6)

If I am Your child, then I won't let anyone deceive me and I will live holy because You are holy. (1 John 3:7)

If you are constantly sinning, then you belong to the devil since sin began with the devil and he constantly keeps sinning. (1 John 3:8)

If I am born again, then I don't constantly sin because I have a new nature that tells me what to do. This is how you tell the difference between a child of God and a child of the devil. If you constantly sin and don't love other Christians, then you are not in God's family. (1 John 3:10)

If I love other Christians, then it proves I have been delivered from death and hell and I have eternal life. (1 John 3:14)

If I refuse to love a believer, then it proves I am just the same as a murderer, and murderers don't have eternal life. (1 John 3:15)

If someone has money and professes to know You, yet refuses to give to a needy Christian, then how could You live in Him? I will not love in words only, I will show my real love by the things I do. (1 John 3:17–18)

If my conscience makes me feel guilty because I sin, then I realize You know everything about me for You are greater than my conscience. (1 John 3:20)

If my conscience doesn't convict me, then I can come to You with my request in prayer to get

what I ask, because I am keeping Your commands. And this is Your commandment that I
believe in the name of Your Son, Jesus Christ;
I love believers as You commanded us. (1 John
3:21–22)

If I keep Your commands, then I know I live in
You, and You live in me. (1 John 3:23)

If every spirit that acknowledges that Jesus Christ
has come in flesh, then it is from You; If every
spirit denies Jesus had a body, then it is not
from You. Those who deny Jesus was human are
Antichrists, who were predicted to come, and are
now here. If Jesus didn't come in a body, then He
couldn't have lived a perfect life, nor could He
have died, nor would He have bled to redeem us,
nor would He have been raised in His physical
body. (1 John 4:2–3)

If I will be victorious over false teaching, then it's
because greater is the Holy Spirit in me than the
spirit of the world. (1 John 4:4)

If those that speak the language of the world get
attention from the world, then they are not from
You. (1 John 4:5)

If I am Your child, then I know You listen to me
and those who belong to You listen to me; this
is how I tell the spirit of truth from the spirit of
falsehood. (1 John 4:6)

If you are born again, then you have been given
the gift of love. (1 John 4:7)

If you fail to love other people, then you have never known Him because He is love. (1 John 4:8)

If You have loved me so much, then I ought to love other believers. (1 John 4:11)

If I love other believers, then you will live in me, and Your love will be seen through me for as long as I love other believers. (1 John 4:12)

If You put the Holy Spirit into my heart, then it is proof that You live in me, and I live in You. (1 John 4:13)

If you acknowledge that Jesus is Your Son, then those who believe live in You, and You in them. (1 John 4:15)

If I know that You love me deeply, then it is because I feel Your love for me. You are love, and whoever lives a life of love, lives in You, and You live in them. (1 John 4:16)

If you do not love, then you are fearful because you do not know what will happen to you in judgment; that proves you are not His child. (1 John 4:18)

If I love You, then it's because You first loved me. (1 John 4:19)

If I say "I love God," but hate a fellow Christian whom I can see, then I cannot love You whom I cannot see. (1 John 4:21)

If anyone loves You, then they must also love his brother or sister. (1 John 4:21)

If I am born again, then it's because I believe Jesus is the Messiah; and all who love You, love Your children also. (1 John 5:1)

If I know I am Your child, it's because I love You and I do what You have commanded me to do. This is what loving You means—keeping Your commands because they are not difficult. (1 John 5:2–3)

If I know I am Your child, then it's because I have victoriously overcome the lust of the world by faith. Only those who believe Jesus is the Son of God can overcome the world. (1 John 5:4–5)

If I know that I am born again, then it's because I have Your witness within. (1 John 5:11)

If everyone believes in Your Son, then they have life; those who reject Your Son make You out to be a liar, but I know I am born again because of Your testimony in Your Word that You have given us Your Son. (1 John 5:12)

If you have the Son, then you have eternal life, and you know you are born again because you have God's Son in your heart. (1 John 5:13)

If I know I am born again, then it's because You hear my prayers, and I know You will answer my prayers because You do not hear and answer the prayers of unsaved people. (1 John 5:15)

If I pray for those who commit a sin that does not lead to death, then You will give them life. (1 John 5:16)

If I know I am born again, then it's because I do not continually practice sin because the Son of God protects me from the evil one. (1 John 5:18)

If I know I am born again, then it's because I realize all non-Christians are lost, but Your children have this spiritual insight. I know the Son of God has come into my heart to give me spiritual understanding to know You, and I know You are the true God who gives eternal life. I will watch out for anything that takes Your place in my heart. (1 John 5:19–21)

Book of 2 John

If we love one another, then we keep His words and commands, which we are urgently reminded is an important principle to follow. (2 John 1:5–6)

If you wander from the teachings of Christ, then you will lose God's influence in your life. (2 John 1:8)

If you remain true to Christian doctrine, then you have both the Father and the Son. (2 John 1:9)

If anyone comes teaching that Jesus Christ is not equal in nature to the Father, then do not receive him or give him hospitality, nor recommend him to other churches because those who support him will become partners in his false teaching. (2 John 1:10–11)

Book of 3 John

If the believers in Your church do right, then they prove they are God's children. (3 John 1:11)

Book of Jude

If you are a Christian, then you need to defend the complete faith that You have once and for all been given, because some have infiltrated the churches who are the ones you have been previously warned about. These people were condemned for denying Your truth and have turned Your freedom into an opportunity to sin, and as a result have rejected the authority of our Master, Jesus Christ. (Jude 1:3)

If you give yourself to sin, then there is punishment in hell for you. (Jude 1:7)

If there are false teachers, then they will mock anything they do not understand and like animals they do anything they feel like doing; by giving into their lusts, their actions become fatal. (Jude 1:10)

If you are a false teacher, then you will get what you deserve and you will be punished. (Jude 1:11)

If you are a false teacher, then you are complainers, malcontents, doing only what your desires—

lusts—drive you to do. You boast and brag about your spirituality, and you give lip service to leaders in the church, but you do it to your advantage. (Jude 1:16)

If there are those who have doubts, then I will have mercy on them and I will try to help those who argue against You. I will point them to You by being kind to them. (Jude 1:22–23)

If I praise You, then it's because You can keep me from falling, and You can deliver me faultless into Your glorious presence so that I am happy and preserved in Christ. (Jude 1:24)

Book of Revelation

If I lose my first love for Him, then I will remember those times when I was first saved and go back to doing what I originally did. (Revelation 2:5)

If you have ears to hear spiritual messages, then listen to what the Holy Spirit is saying to the churches. If you live victorious over sin, then you will eat from the tree of life in Paradise. (Revelation 2:7)

If you have to die for Me, then be faithful for you will receive the crown of life. (Revelation 2:10)

If you have ears to hear spiritual messages, then listen to what the Holy Spirit is saying to the churches. (Revelation 2:11)

If you are victorious, then you have nothing to fear in the second death. (Revelation 2:11)

If you don't repent, then He will come to judge you, with the truth of the Word of God. (Revelation 2:16)

If they have ears to hear spiritual messages, then listen to what the Holy Spirit is saying to the churches. Those who are victorious will receive hidden manna from heaven to strengthen them, and their new names will be engraved on a white stone. And no one knows what it is except those who receive it. (Revelation 2:17)

If a Jezebel woman who entices Christians away from the true faith by getting them to commit adultery and sacrifice to an idol and eat its food, then if she does not repent and change her ways, He will bring suffering to her life, and those who commit adultery with her will suffer intently unless they repent. Her children will die prematurely under judgment, so all churches realize that Jesus continually searches deeply into hearts to give people what their behavior deserves. (Revelation 2:20–23)

If you are victorious and continue serving until the end, then you will receive power over the nations. (Revelation 2:26)

If they have ears to hear spiritual messages, then listen to what the Holy Spirit is saying to the churches. (Revelation 2:29)

If you don't repent and wake up, then Jesus will come unexpectedly to judge you like a thief in the night. (Revelation 3:3)

If they have ears to hear spiritual messages, then listen to what the Holy Spirit is saying to the churches. If you are victorious, then you will be dressed in white. Your name will not be blotted from the Book of Life, and Jesus will acknowledge you to God the Father. (Revelation 3:5–6)

If you wrongly claim to be Christians, then Jesus will judge those in the false church, making them bow at His feet at the Great White Throne Judgment. (Revelation 3:9)

If you have ears to hear spiritual messages, then listen to what the Holy Spirit is saying to the churches. If you are victorious over sin, then Jesus will make you like a pillar in the temple of God, and you will be tested no more. Jesus will write God's name on you, and you will be inhabitants of the New Jerusalem, the city that will come down from God in heaven. (Revelation 3:12–13)

If you are Christians who are lukewarm, then He will spit you out of His mouth. (Revelation 3:16)

If you are claiming to be rich and think you have everything you need, then you don't realize you are wretched, miserably poor, blind, and naked. Jesus warns us to buy from Him gold purified by fire that will make us truly rich, to dress ourselves in righteousness like pure white robes to cover our spiritual nakedness, and to put spiritual ointment on our blinded eyes, so we can have spiritual insight. (Revelation 3:18)

If you hear My voice and open the door when I am knocking, then I will come into spiritually feed you. (Revelation 3:20)

If you are victorious, then you will share the throne of Jesus just as He was victorious over death and took His place at the right hand of the Father. If you have ears to hear, then listen to what the Holy Spirit is saying to the churches. (Revelation 3:21–22)

If we are Christians, then we will rejoice and be glad because the marriage supper of the Lamb is ready. Jesus will be united with His Bride, the church. The Bride is ready because she is made pure by the blood of the Lamb. She is dressed in fine white linen, which is made from the good deeds of the saints. (Revelation 19:7–8)

If you are a saint that is invited to the wedding supper of the Lord, then you are blessed by the Lord. (Revelation 19:9)

If you read the Book of Revelation and believe what it says, then you are blessed. (Revelation 22:7)

If you live by His Word, then you can enter the gates into the city, and eat the fruit of the Tree of Life. But prohibited from the city will be rebels, sorcerers, the sexually impure, murderers, idolaters, and those who love to lie. (Revelation 22:14–15)

If you read this book and add anything too it, then God will add to your punishment. And if you take away from the things in this book, then God will take away your part in the Book of Life and in the holy city. (Revelation 22:18–19)

Thoughts to Ponder

God said, "There shall no man see Me, and live." Yet in heaven, we shall see God's face, the most wonderful thing in heaven that we will see. Today we can't see God, for He is invisible and does not have a body; yet through our prayer, we can enter God's presence to make intercession to Him because we come through the blood of Christ, which makes a way for us.

The great promises that God has given us through Jesus are way beyond what we as humans could think or imagine. His promises to us include freeing us from bondage and slavery to sin. He places us beside Him in heavenly places, and He has given us our identity in Him. There may be times you feel God's promises weren't meant for you, but His promises are always true, and He is faithful in fulfilling them.

Praying God's Word is very powerful because when we pray His Word, we are agreeing with God, and there is power in agreement. God loves when we pray His Word because we honor Him and show Him that we trust that His Word is true. Here is an example of how to pray His Word by making it personal:

> If My people will humble themselves and pray and turn back to Me and away from their sinful ways, I will hear in heaven and forgive them and make their land fertile again. (2 Chronicles 7:14)

Lord, I am Your child, and I will humble myself and pray and will turn back to You and away from my sinful ways. Thank You that You will hear in heaven and forgive me and make my land fertile again, in Jesus's name. Amen.

If you do not know the Promiser and would like to have a personal relationship with Him, not just to receive His promises but to truly know Him intimately, then the "Sample Prayer for Salvation" that appears below can open the door for you to have an eternal relationship with the only Living God who loves you and died for you.

Jesus Christ extends an invitation to *all* who believe in Him and want Him to be their Savior and Lord. It is up to us to accept His invitation.

In the book of John, we are reminded: "For God so loved the world that He gave His one and only Son that whoever believes in Him shall not perish, but have eternal life" (John 3:16).

The book of Romans instructs us "that if you confess with your mouth to the Lord Jesus and believe in your heart that God has raised Him from the dead, you will be saved" (Romans 10:9).

Sample Prayer for Salvation

Lord Jesus, I confess that I am a sinner and need a Savior. I ask You to come into my heart and be my Savior and Lord. I believe that You died on the cross for me so that I can have eternal life with You. I believe that You are the only way to heaven and the only One who forgives my sins. I pray in Jesus's name. Amen.

About the Author

Carol Morris is an ordained minister with a PhD in Christian counseling. She has counseled for eighteen years; taught numerous Bible studies at Monroeville Assembly of God Church; started, organized, and taught at yearly ladies' in-house retreats for the last fifteen years. She also served as an altar worker, organized and served in shut-in and hospital visitation, sang in the church choir for ten years, and held prayer meetings in her home for several years. She has experienced God's miraculous healing for her broken foot, a growth on her vocal chords, and a growth on her ovaries. The growths miraculously disappeared; she went to church on crutches and left without them, fully able to walk on her foot. She came to know the Promiser, Jesus, April 11, 1979, and was baptized in the Holy Spirit. These personal encounters changed her life drastically for the better. She has overcome breast cancer for fourteen years. She has been married for fifty-one years. She enjoys kayaking, biking, taking walks with her husband and her dog, swimming, boating, crossword puzzles, jigsaw puzzles, and reading the Bible, devotionals, and inspirational books.

She was inspired by God, who wants us to understand the way promises are to be made and kept.

CPSIA information can be obtained
at www.ICGtesting.com
Printed in the USA
BVHW070537150921
616751BV00002B/282